Interviews with Mexican Women

Interviews with Mexican Women: We Don't Talk About Feminism Here presents a series of conversations with Mexican women representing a wide geographical range within Mexico. The interviews broach current social issues and discuss their correlation to the Mexican feminist movement of the 1970s and 1980s. This unique project focuses on cultural, political, economic, and social topics as they pertain to Mexican women impacted (or not) by the women's struggle in Mexico to achieve gender equality in their country.

This book offers a rare insight into feminist influence on many areas of social life, and will be a vital text for students and researchers in Gender Studies and Mexican or Latin American Studies.

Carlos M. Coria-Sanchez is an Associate Professor at the University of North Carolina Charlotte in the Languages and Culture Studies Department and in the Latin American Studies Program of which he is Director. He teaches courses in Mexican and Latin American Literature, Latin American Women Writers, and Mexican Women Writers. Dr. Coria-Sanchez has coedited two books published by Yale University Press: *Visiones: Realidades sociales en la literatura Hispana*, Fall 2002; and *Temas del comercio y la economía en la narrativa hispana*, Spring 2008. In 2010 McGraw-Hill published his coauthored text book, *Entre Socios: Español para el mundo profesional*. Also, in 2010, Plaza y Valdez published his book *Angeles Mastretta y el feminismo en México*. In 2016 McFarland & Co. published his coauthored book *Mexican Business Culture: Essays on Tradition, Ethics, Entrepreneurship and Commerce and the State*. More recently, in 2018, Ediciones Eon published his book *Mexicanos al grito de Viva Estados Unidos*. Dr. Coria-Sanchez was the recipient of the Fulbright Scholar Grant in 2008–2009.

Focus on Global Gender and Sexuality

www.routledge.com/Focus-on-Global-Gender-and-Sexuality/book-series/
FGGS

Interviews with Mexican Women

We Don't Talk About Feminism Here

Carlos M. Coria-Sanchez

Routledge
Taylor & Francis Group

LONDON AND NEW YORK

First published 2019
by Routledge
2 Park Square, Milton Park, Abingdon, Oxon OX14 4RN

and by Routledge
605 Third Avenue, New York, NY 10017

First issued in paperback 2020

Routledge is an imprint of the Taylor & Francis Group, an informa business

British Library Cataloguing-in-Publication Data
A catalogue record for this book is available from the British Library

Library of Congress Cataloging-in-Publication Data
A catalog record for this book has been requested

Typeset in Times New Roman
by Apex CoVantage, LLC

ISBN 13: 978-0-367-72883-0 (pbk)
ISBN 13: 978-1-138-58137-1 (hbk)

Contents

Preface

The 1970s and the subsequent decades were of enormous importance to the feminist activist movement in Mexico. It is likely that many upper-middle- to upper-class women may have been influenced by the writings and engagement of women and men involved with the movement during this time. However, it is difficult to trace a visible impact that the feminist ideologies of these years had on middle- to lower-class women. It is possible that these women did not have direct access to the literature associated with the feminist movement or the undertakings that an important portion of the population was carrying out to promote women's rights in many areas of social life – namely, politics, economy, arts, culture, and business – in a nation with a long history of patriarchal dominance.

The interviewees have been chosen arbitrarily through contacts in Mexico. These women belong to different social levels and education; they are in their twenties, thirties, forties, fifties, sixties, or seventies. They are either employed, retired, or housewives, and the interviews include two population types: 1) Mexican women who were young during the fervent years of feminist activity with an analysis of how it affected their lives up to current times, and 2) Mexican women who didn't live through those tumultuous years but whose way of life and thinking have been the final product of the history of the feminist movement. There is not a "questionnaire" *per se*. Instead, an outline of topics is used to create a narrative; the goal is to generate a structured dialogue in which each interviewee feels free to talk about social issues as they pertain to their own firsthand experiences in Mexico during the feminist movement and thereafter. It is important to note that most of the interviews were conducted in Spanish and translated into English; however, once aware that this was a book to be published in English, some of the interviewees decided to speak in this language instead of having their narratives translated. Accordingly, minor editing has been done to these interviews.

Acknowledgments

I would like to express my gratitude to the following people for their help with some of the interviews: Olivia Daniela Garcia, John Hyatt, and Nashaly Ruiz-Gonzalez. Also, as always, my gratitude to my wife Karyn for her support throughout the process of writing this book, for reading it and for her insightful suggestions and comments. A special thank you to all those brave Mexican women who generously shared their stories with me for this project – they are the real authors. I love my sons Alberto, Pablo, and Oliver. I couldn't have a better family.

1 Introduction

Before talking about Mexican women's rights, it is important to remember that the 1970s was a decade of a strong women's civil liberties movement in Mexico that influenced other neighboring countries as well. The Mexican feminist movement of this era hosted the first International Women's Conference in Mexico City in 1975 that attracted women and organizations from all over the world. This symposium was one of many social events that illustrate the great significance of the feminist movement in the nation.

The 1970s was a time of multiple social struggles for economic, political, cultural, and educational rights for women throughout Mexico. During this decade and the ones that followed, a myriad of women wrote and openly denounced oppressive social conditions via what would come to be considered the most important and oldest feminist magazine in the country and in Latin America: *FEM*. Women wrote about issues such as school education, sex education, marriage, housework, art, culture, and society in general in a country with a long history of patriarchal non-written rules that disadvantaged women. At first *FEM* was perceived as an elitist journal for those who belonged to the academic community and for the upper-middle to upper classes since it was hardly read by middle- and working-class women. However, the journal was one more contributing element in the complex set of dynamics that raised consciousness in millions of women about their subordinate status under a male-ruled Mexican society. These years also saw the rise of important Mexican female writers like Angeles Mastretta, Ethel Krauze, Laura Esquivel, and Brianda Domecq, among others, who clearly identified themselves with the feminist movement in the country, and who tried to influence their readers through their works: novels, short stories, plays, essays, and poetry.

FEM did not stick to any specific feminist ideology; however, many of the writers in the journal translated or followed up on theoretical essays written in other countries, mainly European nations and the United States, complementing them with their own cultural and historical circumstances

regarding women's rights. Regrettably, to this day there is no fully artic-
ulated Mexican or Latin American feminist theory to decipher women's
status in society in an extremely diverse continent. Nevertheless, some phi-
losophers like Ofelia Shutte have written extensively on the topic. Shutte
can be credited with a deeper explanation of the causes that may have led to
Latin American women's historical and cultural subjugation in the region.
In the case of Mexico, many scholars only look at American and European
feminist theories to define Mexican women's oppression and struggles. The
works and critical essays of these academicians have relied traditionally
on the philosophies of liberal, radical, Marxist, and postmodern feminism.
As stated, there is no well-established autochthonous Latin American feminist theory, that is, a Latin American feminist theory born out of the very
social context that the theory should explain. As Debra Castillo says, many
Latin American feminist critics have put American and European theories
in a blender and mixed them up to explain the situation of women in Latin
America. The following is a brief examination of some of these hybrid
ideologies.

2 Feminist perspectives

It is appropriate to raise the question of whether it is true that the feminist movement exists as the "global" conscience of the emancipation of women. This question has given rise to a complex debate in contemporary societies. It is true that the origin of the feminist movement united a substantial number of women in the struggle against political, economic, and social marginalization and subordination in patriarchal societies. The multiplicity of feminist theories, each seeking the causes and effects of, and solutions to the oppression of women, however, could be perceived as creating more rupture than convergence among feminist women and men.

Each feminist theory considers itself the representative of the truth. Be it termed liberal, Marxist, radical, postmodern, or other, it is certain that each feminist perspective aims to describe the oppression of women. Nevertheless, many consider it doubtful that these theories may have been informed by historical and cultural contexts pertaining to different societies in which women live. These theories do try to explain women's subordination, its causes, and the best path forward for women's liberation. Nonetheless, they are only a provisional answer to the global concerns for women's rights.

1.1 Liberal feminism

Liberal feminist theory considers "gender" to be the source of women's subordination and the impediment to their access to "the world of men." Liberal feminist theory arose in the nineteenth century, represented by Mary Wollstonecraft and John Stuart Mill, among others. Founded on the ideas of the French Revolution of liberty and equality, this theory stresses that women must have the same opportunities as men in the workplace, in education, and in politics through participation in government and other institutions.

Liberal feminism insists that women be given the opportunity to develop as individuals engaged in public life of their country, a domain that has belonged only to men. To such effect, women should go out and fight against the structures that oppress them and restrict their public life. Mill points out that "the general opinion of men is supposed to be that the natural vocation of women is that of wife and mother" (157),[1] an attitude that, per the liberal position, should be eradicated from society. Later, during the twentieth century, liberal feminism struggled against marriage and motherhood as institutions created by patriarchal societies, whose social norms are oppressive to women.

The liberal feminist movement points out that the oppression and subordination of women is the product of norms based on "gender." Liberal feminists, as viewed by Allison Jaggar and Paula Rothenberg, "Aspire to the freeing of women from oppressive gender roles, ones that throughout history have placed them in inferior positions. Liberal feminist activism is therefore directed toward criticizing the injustice of those norms and working towards changing them" (117).[2] It is important to note that liberal feminism in not interested in changing the basic governing structure of society; it wants to include women in this structure, and allow them to participate in all areas of society.

1.2 Marxist feminism

While gender is at the center of liberal feminist theory, Marxist feminist theory rejects the notion of "gender" and that of biological determinism and maintains that class differences within capitalist society are the root of women's oppression. Tong mentions that, in general, Marxist feminism sees capitalism as a system of exploitation where the profits generated by a large poor majority end up in the hands of a rich minority. Women supply future workers in addition to providing clothing, food, clean and comfortable housing, and offering emotional support to existing workers.[3]

Marxist feminists think that women are not actually victims of men, but victims of the oppression created by class differences. Marxist feminism invites every woman, regardless of social class, to understand women's oppression as the product of political, social, and economic structures associated with the capitalist system.

The liberation of women, for the Marxist feminist movement, can be achieved only through the elimination of the capitalist system. At variance with the ideas of liberal feminism and those of radical feminism, Marxist feminist theory approaches the oppression, subordination, and liberation of women from the standpoint of capitalism. Proponents of Marxist feminist theory maintain that the system cannot be abolished solely by women, but by means of a worldwide struggle led by the working class – women and men.

1.3 Radical feminism

In contrast to Marxist feminist theory, radical feminism maintains that the oppression of women is the most fundamental of all forms of oppression, and that it cannot be eradicated altogether by means of other social changes such as the elimination of capitalism. The oppression of women is not merely oppression based on social class.

Rejecting the Marxist position of class struggle, radical feminist theory insists on reestablishing the male as the oppressor who upholds female subordination, not the capitalist system. Criticism of the patriarchal system also derives from the way in which marriage and motherhood have been created as two modes of oppression that subjugate women and consider them to be reproductive, not productive, beings within society. In this respect, Shulamite Firestone points out that reproductive relations are the driving forces in history. If we want to understand why women are subordinated to men, we require a biological, not an economic, explanation (56).[4]

For radical feminists, then, eradication of the oppression and subordination of women cannot be realized by merely abolishing legal and political institutions. The dismantling of these institutions needs to be coupled with eliminating social and cultural institutions such as the family and the church, as well as the academic world.

1.4 Postmodern feminism

On the other hand, we have postmodern feminist theory. Until recently, postmodern feminism was known as French feminism since many of its proponents are either French, live in, or lived in France. Some of the most noted adherents of this discourse are Helene Cixous, Luce Irigaray, and Julia Kristeva.

Many of the roots of postmodern feminism can be found in Simone de Beauvoir's *The Second Sex*. Beauvoir's idea of "the Other" is taken up anew by this group of feminists. Subverting the original notions of inferiority and marginality of women by casting them as "the second sex," postmodern feminists reclaim the "second sex" advantages. In other words, postmodern feminism does not interpret "the Other" as a shortcoming; on the contrary, this "Otherness" allows women to fire back and make a critique of the values that patriarchy imposes on all those who live outside the center, that is, in the periphery.

With the direct influence of French thinkers like Jacques Lacan and Jacques Derrida, and the latter's methods of deconstruction, Cixous, Irigaray, and Kristeva problematize and deconstruct language with the intention of dismantling the masculine parameters under which natural languages have been created. The problematization and deconstruction of the function of language, as a reflection of Lacan's Symbolic Order, provide a key to understanding the real objective of postmodern feminist theory.

Thus, postmodern feminism is based on the premise of problematizing and deconstructing the Symbolic Order – that is, society and the entire system of norms created by men. In his examination of the Symbolic Order and its social implications, Jacques Lacan observes language as the medium through which an individual adapts to the norms dictated by society and the way in which that individual functions within it. The Symbolic Order imposed by language as a social regulator represses women as social individuals.

Irigaray, in *This Sex Which Is Not One*, uses her writing to deconstruct the cultural representations that have been created around women based on masculine parameters. Irigaray suggests that the goal of feminist discourse is the destruction of masculine models to give way to a different Symbolic Order – a Symbolic Order that seeks, finds, and reflects an authentic femininity.

The criticism that emerges from postmodern feminist texts suggests a problematization and deconstruction of the Symbolic Order that, built on phallocentric structures, oppresses and marginalizes women. Postmodern feminism, then, seeks a freedom that is fundamental for the total liberation of women, that is, freedom from imposed thought and language.

As we can see from this range of feminist theories, each tends to give priority to certain factors as the original cause of women's oppression. The evolution of each of these theories presents its own perspectives, responses, or solutions, as well as its own justifications in the struggle for women's liberation. However, there are points in which all the theories coincide. One of these, and possibly the most important one, is the problematization of the real causes of the oppression of women, for which we must take into consideration the cultural, historical, and economic contexts of present-day societies.

The existence of several different feminist theories allows us to analyze not only the differences that exist between men and women in society, but also the differences that exist among women themselves. One imperative should not be overlooked from the origin of the women's liberation movement. As Marta Lamas explains in the journal *NEXOS*, "the feminist goal is not that men and women will be happy in a symmetrical world, but rather that we will be happy when the differences that exist between men and women no longer signify inequality" (this author's translation) (*"el planteamiento feminista no es el de que los hombres y las mujeres seremos felices en un mundo simétrico, sino más bien, que lo seremos cuando la diferencia entre los hombres y las mujeres no signifique desigualdad"*).

1.5 Intersectionality

Intersectionality[5] has become one of the most important feminist theories of the last 30 years since Kimberly Crenshaw formulated the idea in 1989. Crenshaw used the concept of intersectionality to discuss how gender, race, and class interact to demonstrate how the confluence of these issues creates a social disadvantage for women from various backgrounds. Intersectionality focuses on the social inequalities within social structures according to each woman's individual context, which is closely linked to social, cultural, and political practices.

The focus of intersectionality became, in the last decades, an important word in the English-speaking feminist world, because it is, according to its proponents, the normal development of the non-hegemonic feminism that since the '70s has questioned the white, heterosexual, middle-class perspective.

Intersectionality's attention is to analyze the formal and informal processes that create social inequalities. This focus reveals that such inequalities are the result of the interactions between subordination in terms of gender, sexual orientation, ethnic background, religion, national origin, and socio-economic status as well as sexism, racism, and classism, all of which can contribute to women's discrimination and suffering.

Intersectionality deals with issues that are still open in feminist debates that were and still are relevant for the feminist movement in general. Its novelty resides in its emphasis on the discrimination and privileges obtained by some based on gender, sexual orientation, ethnic background, religion, national origin, and socio-economic status.

Intersectionality finds its origins in African American feminism, which has criticized the concept of gender based only on the standardized experience of white middle-class women without taking into consideration other social factors such as race, class, or sexual orientation. African American feminism criticizes the white hegemonic feminist discourse which presumes to speak for all women assuming their universalism and neutrality. However, their discourse is built under the assumption that all women share the same characteristics as those of the dominant group. White women, however unintentional it may have been, created generalizations based on their own heterosexual, Christian, middle-class status, which basically ignored women with different social, racial, and ethnic backgrounds. The main reason to find an explanation from African American, Chicana, and post-colonial feminism is to recreate an origin about the concept of intersectionality, which aims to show that its genealogy is linked to the development and practice of non-hegemonic feminism. These characteristics, unique in American history, were the bases upon which the concept of intersectionality came about.[6]

It would not be absurd to think that Mexican women would fall into this newer feminist theory to explain their own social, political, cultural discrimination in a country where class and ethnic origin also play an important role when it comes to women's status within society. Like their Anglo-Saxon counterparts, Mexican middle-upper-class and upper-class feminists, light skinned, and well educated, may have disregarded the struggle for social rights and justice that, for instance, indigenous women from different historical and geographical backgrounds have endured for centuries.

Notes

1 Mills, John Stuart. "The Subjection of Women." *Feminist Frameworks*. Eds. Alison Jaggar and Paula Rothenberg. McGraw-Hill, 1993.
2 Jaggar, Allison and Paula Rothenberg. "Theories of Women's Subordination." *Feminist Frameworks*. Eds. Alison Jaggar and Paula Rothenberg. McGraw-Hill, 1993.
3 Tong, Rosemarie. *Feminist Thought*. Westview Press, 2009.
4 Firestone, Shulamite. "The Culture of Romance." *Feminist Frameworks*. Eds. Alison Jaggar and Paula Rothenberg. McGraw-Hill, 1993.
5 La Barbera, Maria Caterina. "Interseccionalidad, un 'concepto viajero': orígenes, desarrollo e implementacion en la Union Europea." *Interdisciplina* 4, No. 8 (2016): 105–122.
6 *Ibid.*

3 The Mexican context

It wouldn't be difficult to establish that working-class Mexicans have been attracted to leftist ideas, namely those arising from a Marxist ideology. There is a long history of Mexican class struggle as it can be observed, for instance, during the Mexican Revolution when the poor urban workers and peasants fought for better social conditions and a better life. The incipient Mexican capitalist system subjugated peasants and workers alike under precarious conditions creating a movement that didn't end with the official close of the Mexican Revolution on November 20, 1920. On the contrary, class struggle has been an ongoing crusade for the duration of the country's history. During these many decades of social unrest, women have fought alongside men to achieve a more just system and better economic conditions for themselves and their families.

The triumph of the Russian Revolution in 1917 initiated a series of changes around the world between two ideologies: socialism and capitalism. These events had quick repercussions in Mexico where the Mexican communist party held congresses in various parts of the country led by people such as the Flores Magón brothers, who showed their admiration and support for the October Revolution. There were, also, detractors who accused any demonstrations or workers' marches as purely communist and Bolshevik.

Mexican women were viewed as a sector that could be brought in to fight for social reforms in the country. The communist party believed that with the creation of organizations of middle-class female employees, workers, and peasants there was a way to pay attention to women's issues and their social oppression under a patriarchal rule, but the final objective was for women to join and participate in the country's class struggles in general. That is the reason why from the beginning, women in the party created political organizations and unions that would function as a link between the women's masses and the communist party. The communist party maintained that women's political participation remained within the framework of the social class struggle inside the program and objectives of the party. In this way, they would consolidate all their efforts for the social fight against the capitalist system.[1]

For many leaders within the communist party something was clear from the start: the feminine front of the party differed from feminism, which some believed was bourgeois and reactionary. According to certain communist beliefs, feminism endeavored to separate women from men and prevented the former from participating in the class struggle. Feminism was individualistic, and women's revolutionary fight required a spirit of class struggle without selfish or individual concerns against a system that kept the poor poorer and the rich richer. It wasn't a gender fight but a social class struggle. Communist women attempted to combat feminists and tried to exclude them from the communist party. These two fractions continued to confront each other throughout the years; however, despite their antagonistic ideological positions, both participated in the communist party.

Mexican communist women emphasized that the participation of many other women in the industrial and rural sectors in the class struggle against Mexican bourgeoise and American imperialism was growing in the country. For that reason, the party supported the creation of women's revolutionary organizations and unions led by workers and peasants. The party's goal was to bring together all Mexican women to fight for female workers' rights.

In the 1970s, Mexico witnessed terrible economic instability. The peso's devaluation increased unemployment, and women were the first to suffer this crisis; they were laid off in the thousands around the country. Women were viewed as "less educated than men" or less productive than men in the long run due to inevitable pregnancy, in which case, it was thought, the companies would lose money. The 1980s brought another severe crisis to the country which became known as "The Lost Decade in Latin America." Mexico was stricken by many economic crises that afflicted multiple nations from south of the Rio Grande all the way to Argentina. Again, there were masses of unemployed people with women being the most affected demographic group. These crises demanded that women take a more active role in the country's workforce for their families' well-being.

The feminist movement of the 1970s and 1980s in Mexico was the outcome of the economic crises in the country. Women were looking, through these groups, for a way to act and transform the system's political and economic structure to win a new social position in society. It became a priority for women to join the spheres of power and the socio-economic and political life of the country. The 1970s had been a decade of intense political and social activity for Mexican women. The economic crises the country went through triggered a strong insurgence of unions in which women were the main protagonists. Several strikes around the country were led by women:

in 1971 in the clothing factory "Medalla de oro"; in 1975 the international company Spicer went on strike as well; in 1977 several university workers around the country did the same; in 1978 the furniture factory DM Nacional closed due to another strike; and in 1979 telephone company operators went on strike as well. These were only some of the most important and transcendental union political actions in the country. Women's presence in the social and political movements of the country was of vital importance. Of note are the urban popular movement of 1973 in Monterrey, the street vendors movement in 1973 in Mexico City, and the women's union workers in the National Autonomous University of Mexico (UNAM) in 1976, just to mention a few.[2]

The Mexican feminist movement of the 1970s became known as the new wave of feminism. This rebirth of feminism in the country was the idea of a group of women concerned about the lack of opportunities for women to participate in Mexican social, political, cultural life, and more importantly, to make decisions about their own bodies and problems inherent to them as women. Most of these women were urban, middle class, and college students or professors who lived in Mexico City. Many events had to take place for women of this era to realize the oppressive system under which they lived, and to begin a struggle to transform the system: a vast number of women entering the workforce, more women attending schools, and the influence of feminist movements from other countries, especially the United States. There were attempts to unify ideas and women in a common front, but they failed. Homosexual feminists, for instance, felt they were discriminated against or not considered by other women. During the earthquake of 1985 in which many female workers were killed in locked sweatshops with no escape, the feminist movement finally understood that they hadn't taken into consideration low-working-class women as part of their fight for rights. No one had paid any attention to these women workers' ideology, needs, and concerns, which differed from those of the upper-middle and upper classes.

On the other hand, there were indigenous women's protests for better living conditions around the country, especially in the area which is now known as the EZLN (Zapatist Army of National Liberation). Through these movements, indigenous women denounced the feminist program in the country, that it had not taken them into account regarding their own needs, social and political demands, or their cultural and historical background. In other words, they didn't exist for the Mexican feminist agenda; they were invisible as were the working-class women of urban areas.

Although there are no direct links between Marxist feminist theory and the Mexican feminist movement of the '70s and '80s, we can trace a parallel that shows that the social concerns, fights, and political activism that working-class, peasants, and some middle-class women were involved in are within the main ideas of the Marxist ideology of class struggle. This struggle of workers and indigenous communities was against the capitalist system and neo-liberal economic policies that the Mexican government applies to the country where more than 50% of the population lives under the poverty line. These women fighting and organizing alongside men may not think that they are gender victims *per se*, but rather, they see themselves as oppressed by the social, political, and economic structures of the capitalist system that creates these class differences.

So, how can we identify the impact that women's rights discourse had on the "common" Mexican woman? We know that the needs of middle- and upper-class Mexican women differ greatly from those in lower classes. The latter face challenges that are not experienced by the former, such as the lack of well-paid jobs, housing, and access to education; hunger; addictions; not to mention the lack of participation in politics, culture, and arts in society.

It is justified to ask if the feminist movement really had an impact on more "common" Mexican women who didn't belong to academia or didn't have direct access to feminist literature. Therefore, the analysis of their testimony may shed light on to what extent the movement for equal rights in Mexico affected their lives in any significant way.

Many working-class women in Mexico are still subject to verbal, physical, and sexual abuse. Those in urban areas stop going to school in early high school because they must begin contributing to their family finances; it is even worse for women in rural areas, where many times women only have two or three years of education and tend to the agricultural fields or hold low-paying jobs in their communities; therefore, they migrate to the big cosmopolitan cities (or the United States) to work in factories or as maids. Many women from these social strata face a societal barrier that does not allow them to participate in society in general. A vast number of these women marry at an early age and begin child-rearing as early as 14 or 15 years old with a partner or husband who does not share with them the same responsibilities and rights. The question, then, would be if at any time these women were aware of the new feminist movement in Mexico, in the big cities or rural communities, and if the movement taught them to organize and to fight for their rights.

Mexican women, single or married, often migrate to big cities like Mexico City, Guadalajara, Monterrey, Puebla, and Veracruz out of necessity and to improve their lives and those of their families. Do these women experience more freedom in what is supposed to be a more open society? Do they learn from other women, some of them progressive feminists, to share more with their partners/husbands or do they remain as the "women of the house" with all the responsibilities that this conveys? Do they learn from other women to fight for their rights? Do they keep their original traditions as mothers and wives?

There are many questions to answer about these women who lived during and after the active years of the Mexican feminist movement that spanned several decades beginning with the 1970s. The best way to learn about their experiences in Mexico is by allowing them to create their own narrative. The main idea behind this book is to interview women in cities like Mexico City, Guadalajara, Monterrey, and Puebla. Through informal conversations with these women, we will learn about their social status and living conditions in Mexico subsequent to the tumultuous times of the country's feminist movement.

Notes

1 Reyes Castellanos, Francisca. *Sembradoras de futuros: memoria de la unión nacional de mujeres mexicanas*. Unión Nacional de Mujeres Mexicanas, A.C., 2000.
2 Coria-Sánchez, Carlos M. *Ángeles Mastretta y el feminismo en México*. Plaza y Valdés, 2010.

4   Interviews

Interview 1: Olivia, 36 years old, college instructor and business owner

To me, feminism is a political concept created some generations ago that arose from a state of inequality towards women. This inequality still exists today due to a patriarchal ideology that for years has been feeding a culture based on political interests that benefit only the privileged. It seems to me that in social sectors such as politics and education, our culture and collective consciousness about the lack of inclusive perspectives has been spreading to all kinds of people, not only to women, but to the cause of unequal rights and responsibilities for many. Feminism has gone through some sort of reconstruction according to our times. This has allowed feminism to transcend gender and sex, that is, transcend the biological aspect, and take a more symbolic route. For me there isn't a significant difference between the diverse feminists' movements and those of homosexuals or slaves, because all of these movements draw attention to each group's condition as citizens who would like to live a full life.

I define myself as more of an inclusive person than a feminist. I defend everyone's rights to be seen and respected, and to participate in a free and democratic life according to their own ideals without being judged. I think that no concept should exist that creates differences or preferences, much less create biological characteristics that evaluate one's capacities, one's ability to deserve recognition, or one's access to living conditions. In my opinion, to position myself as a feminist reduces my field of action, because I'd like to consider other issues such as diversity and inclusiveness. In this way, I can include not only women's issues, but those of men as well as others who may have a feminine ideology such as homosexuals and transsexuals, or other groups discriminated against on the basis of sexual orientation or physical, mental, and emotional differences.

With regards to previous feminist movements in Mexico like that of the 1970s and 1980s, I know that from a legal standpoint it was possible to do something about women's rights. People became more aware of what women are capable of and began to hear their voices on issues like the right to vote, the right to decide about their own bodies, both sexually and in reproductive ways, and the right to get legal help in cases of violence against them. There were very important cultural advances as well. Also, as it happens with any organizations, in these feminist organizations of the '70s and '80s, there were personal interests and dissimilar perspectives that weakened the different fronts for women. To this day, I have met women who, even though they don't call themselves feminists, and who don't belong to such organizations, act to help other women day in and day out without considering age, work, economic status, social or political affiliation. These women teach other women with financial problems, or share knowledge of traditional medicine to create an interconnected sense of community. Of course, I also know of non-profit organizations, civic associations, and isolated groups that openly support feminist causes – for instance, they target small business women owners; other organizations research how women are seen in society; and others, through their journalistic work, research and denounce radical feminism of previous years.

I don't think Mexican women enjoy the same rights as men. It has been necessary to appeal to international human rights organizations to stop the arbitrary atrocities against women that have been taken place in Mexico for the last 20 years starting in Ciudad Juarez and that have since permeated the entire country.

Without a group of organized women fighting for their rights, it wouldn't have been possible to attain equal conditions for all citizens. It was because of their demands and experiences that there are better conditions concerning the law, employment, and the ability to choose one's own way of living. However, contrary to the saying that behind a great man there is a great woman, behind a great woman there is also a great man, who, believing in equal rights, fought alongside her, shoulder to shoulder, fighting for equality in academia, in business firms, and participating in strikes – men who always valued the importance of women's presence in the world. Therefore, I think that rather than herald only one feminist group (which, in themselves, have indeed achieved significant advances), I suggest we acknowledge that there were other types of alliances, of men and women, who defended the right of a human being to be recognized in all his/her dimensions.

Regarding the laws governing the workplace in Mexico, for some years now, there has been more equality in workplace activities, positions, and salaries, especially within international companies. There has also been a gender balance in politics, within the Senate and the House of Representatives. As far as employee benefits for working women, childbirth is covered by the law. However, there are obstacles for a woman to get a job if she is pregnant at the time of applying for a position (employers ask if a woman is pregnant during the interview process). Also, unfortunately, there are too many macho men in large companies who seduce their female employees. Some of them harass women without any repercussions while authorities look the other way. Regarding harassment in the private sector, in many cases, certain women looking for promotions dismiss others' claims of harassment with sexist and misogynous comments. Women, in fact, have worked to be more visible and to participate in different areas of society; however, they often perpetrate illegal and dishonest actions for fear of being fired. Once in power, these women forget to create a sense of community by sharing their gender's circumstances.

I think that women have had success in the field of education because it isn't an area that correlates to social impediment. In general, many women choose certain majors out of vocation. It is possible that some women may have some obstacles at home for having chosen non-traditional majors, and some families may become disappointed because they didn't follow the family tradition in a specific profession. However, I think that Mexico has become more open-minded with regards to professions that women want to pursue. There are generations of parents who understand present-day job needs and the necessity for their daughters to keep improving themselves; that is why these parents give their kids more freedom to decide regardless of their gender.

Concerning sexual freedom, there are States and small regions in Mexico where religious beliefs still govern the teaching of punishment or reward. Religion has been an instrument to threaten those who would be tempted to have a sex partner out of wedlock, or to celebrate those who decide to wait until they get married in the "eyes of God" before establishing a complete relationship with their partner. The lack of sexual freedom and the repercussions of this on the behavior of young people also takes place on a larger scale in more developed cities with large populations. It is in these places where there are more opportunities to mislead others. There are deceitful situations where someone shows one face before the family, and, when no one is looking, shows a different one with friends and partners. These ambiguous behaviors affect women who feel that they must justify their acts, especially if it is in relation to their partner and even if they are married. I think that three generations after I was born, young women will grow up in an environment influenced by their contact with other cultures' mentalities, with TV shows, and with access to the internet – trends that have modified taboos they grew up with. A woman's ability to decide her own sexual preferences depends on the quality of interaction established between the family members, the representation of marriage by the parents, and her education.

As far as traditional roles for women in society, it wasn't too many years ago that there was a movement to leave domestic life for a professional one. This movement raised criticism from those who claimed that women's work at home is a virtue that couldn't be lost. However, this idea changed when reality showed that a woman should not only stay at home to take care of her family, but that she had to support her family economically as well. Even though a woman's role in the family has evolved, there are two topics that still create turmoil in our society – a woman's decision about her own body (abortion) on one hand, and on the other hand, to have a family with a member of the same sex. Both topics have been broadly discussed, have brought much prejudice and ignorance to the surface, and have underlined the conservative influence of the church over a substantial number of the population.

There are Mexican women writers who I know that identify themselves as feminist. Laura Lecona is a writer, editor, and feminist activist within a radical platform. Liliana Zaragoza, writer and photographer has a specialty in human rights. Raquel Castro is not as well known but works on the re-vindication of feminist power throughout her stories. Carmen Aristegu is a journalist and feminist activist.

My education at home was an open one in the sense that I didn't get strong "suggestions" about my activities. I never heard of differences between men and women, only physical ones but nothing else. That is why I remember that since I was a little girl my relationships with boys and girls from my neighborhood and school were the same. My childhood was a period of creativity, of playing with dolls or skateboards. There wasn't a predisposition or prejudice toward certain toys, clothes, or colors, nothing. I was a girl who had too many accidents because I was always climbing trees. It was my school education that showed me that many of my female friends played like girls and liked to pretend to have babies or applied a lot of makeup to look beautiful to attract a boyfriend. When I grew up, my parents showed no tendencies to prohibit me from studying any major I wanted. On the contrary, my parents provided me with plenty of freedom to decide on whatever made me happy, and they helped me to achieve my full potential.

A complicated issue for my parents at the end of college was for me to go live in another city and become independent. Even harder for them was the idea of my boyfriend and I living together. Not too much time passed before I got married after that; however, that prejudice was always present in my parents' minds who, back then, were affected by thinking that I wasn't following the church precepts about couples living together before marriage.

My mother always talked to me about sexuality. Every time I came to her asking about something that I had heard at school, she always made sure about the context in which it had been said. She would ask me what I had understood from that, and then she gave me a simple and honest answer that didn't make room for any doubts. My mom always made up stories that she told my sister and me about how to take care of ourselves, to look out for other people's intentions towards us, and to keep an eye on each other. It was at school that we talked about sex topics in classes like biology, and the older we became, the more often we would discuss the topic. It wasn't until I had a formal boyfriend that my mom talked to me in detail about the subject, without bans or threats, but with a strong emphasis on sexually transmitted diseases, babies, and the different risks that come with having a committed relationship. Those were very understandable discussions that weighed heavily on me emotionally.

Mexican society is matriarchal; however, there are too many machos in certain families. The religious connotations that I have mentioned before have been a taboo that has influenced the way families develop and define roles within the family. The belief in the Virgin of Guadalupe says that all Mexicans are Guadalupians; that is, that she is the mother of all Mexicans. This instills a character of superiority in men in this society. And if men were educated in their family under this model, they never stopped seeing themselves as the sons who depend on and must be served by the women of the house, mother and sisters. This family model is part of the typical Mexican macho who tries in any feasible way to show his manhood. Since childhood, the macho always had a secondary role in the family, and now he wants to prove himself. Of course, not all families are the same. There are kids who were lucky enough to be raised by parents who never made any distinctions between the siblings, and along the way these kids have learned how to respect differences in people. There are parents who have given themselves the opportunity to keep up with their studies, to learn on their own, watch movies, have conversations with others, surf the internet, and so they are more open-minded to whatever is new and different. My former partner grew up within a family that had both traditional and modern practices; however, because he was the youngest, certain traditions were less demanding of him. On the other hand, his professional life allowed him to be more progressive about men's and women's responsibilities. This relationship was always a balanced one; we were supportive of each other and shared everything equally. Sometimes I oversaw mechanical issues for the car, and sometimes he oversaw the preparing of meals at home, for instance.

At home, we don't talk about women's rights the same way we talk about children's rights or any other group's rights. There must be news or something that triggers the conversation in that direction; otherwise we don't mention women's rights at all.

I would like for future girls and boys to inherit a society where they know what their mothers, aunts, and grandmothers have done for social justice. Future boys and girls without taboos; they should be little creative people, willing to collaborate in projects that are inclusive, diverse, that promote respect and togetherness, and solve conflict through peaceful means. I would like for them to be able, regardless of their gender or sex, to work with both masculine and feminine energies to achieve a balance within themselves.

Interview 2: Gabriela, 33 years old, elementary school teacher

I consider feminism to be a movement that has been taking place throughout history and where women have tried to search for gender equality with men as well as in life in general. I personally think of myself as a feminist because I truly believe that women should be treated with the same rights as men. Inequality in the country we live in (Mexico) is primarily patriarchal and macho, a place where men get better economic and social benefits than women; and many times, these issues are not related at all to the skills and knowledge that women or men have.

Feminism has seen some significant advances in our country due to demonstrations, television campaigns, social networking, and open denunciations by feminist women. However, feminism has not attained prominent levels of equality with men because society itself keeps dictating social behavior for women that is difficult to eradicate. Also, our government's inefficiency renders it incapable of completely defending all women's rights.

I believe that without the different feminist movements led by women demanding equality and the same opportunities as men, the country would still be under the same social conditions as before. Women have gained the rights to do many things today thanks to those movements. I think that in comparison to last century and even to a few years ago, there is more balance in the rights and responsibilities that men and women share. These rights and responsibilities pertain to access to higher education where, in the past, women were not allowed to study or work and improve themselves professionally. These days many women share roles and responsibilities equally with their partners in their marriages, they can cast a vote during elections, they can take part in politics with positions that women never had before, practice sports, etc. Little by little spaces are opening for women in social, cultural, educational, and other areas where it was unthinkable for them to participate in the past.

When it comes to education, I think that there are more opportunities for women nowadays; even within those professions considered for "men." However, the way we think, our culture, ideology, religion, etc., continues to communicate to us certain "correct" or "adequate" professions that men and women should follow.

Likewise, I consider that women in Mexico still lack sexual freedom to have the kind of life they would like; that is because we are still subject to opinions and social and religious perceptions about what women should or should not do about this issue. A woman is judged in a pejorative way; she might be called names such as a "bad" woman, even a prostitute many times. There is a very macho vision about this topic in the country.

There is a lot of social influence over the traditional roles that men and women must play in society; for instance, at the end of their higher education studies, women must become housewives, get married, have children, and take care of the children all the time. Men are viewed as the breadwinners of the house and the ones to have a job; this is for men to have more opportunities to improve themselves professionally. However, even though I consider that there is still this kind of social influence, there are some sectors of the population in society that try out different options. There are couples living together without getting married, without kids, where both the man and the woman have a job. This is a tendency that is, bit by bit, getting stronger and where gender roles are becoming interchangeable, more equitable.

Two people come to mind when I think of feminist writers. One is the well-known writer Rosario Castellanos and the other one is the activist Marta Lamas. They have influenced many other women to fight for their rights in the workplace and in other areas of society. Through their writings, conferences, and projects, these two women have created a consciousness in many other women who find themselves in violent or discriminatory situations.

I personally had a traditional Mexican upbringing. Nothing was imposed on me; however, in a subtle way I have taken in many of my parents' ideologies, especially from my mom. She has helped me to form my perception (as if I had been a man) about many topics for which I didn't have a lot of freedom traditionally in our society. My mom, for instance, was always more open-minded (especially because she didn't have a certain religion to rule her life) and this allowed her to be more flexible in many aspects related to gender roles and women's responsibilities. That's why when it came to sexual topics, she always had a direct and open communication towards me, with confidence and love. Since I was a little girl my mom always explained topics about sex to me. However, in that same way, she transmitted her fears and insecurities to me about sex and sexuality. I am totally in favor of open communication between parents and children, without prejudice, fears, and insecurities because in this way we can avoid many bad situations in the future.

I think Mexican society is somewhat patriarchal because *machismo*, as a cultural base, permeates many aspects and levels of society. In my personal life, my partner is a man who is very sensitive to all my needs, he is empathetic, and someone who, from the beginning of our relationship, has been a person who supports all my decisions, whatever they are. He wants me to fulfill my potential both professionally and personally. Communication is very important and is based on trust and respect, considering the rights and responsibilities that each one of us has as an individual and as a couple.

I would like to finish by saying that Mexico still has a lot to do with regards to finding balance and equality between men and women, but thanks to all the movements and work done by many women every day, we are achieving important and relevant changes.

In the future, if I have daughters, I would like them to grow up free, in an environment with equal conditions in all senses. I would like them to be conscious about themselves, and I would hope that this country (Mexico) would have the same rights for everyone. But for that to happen, we must start at home, raising kids with love, imparting a respect for differences, instilling a disrespect for discrimination, and modeling equal inclusiveness for everyone.

Interview 3: Lucila, 67 years old, housewife

I don't know what feminism is. I have heard the word, but I don't know what it means. I associate the word feminism with women. I don't consider myself a feminist because I don't know the concept, but if feminism fights for women's rights, then I do consider myself to be a feminist because I agree with women fighting for their rights. I would like for women to have the same rights as men.

I don't know anything about the Mexican feminist movement from the '70s and '80s. I don't remember anything. I know some women who fight for women's rights like Elena Poniatowska, Angeles Mastretta, and Guadalupe Loaeza, who is a writer. However, I don't remember anything about the movement from the '70s and '80s.

I think that feminism has helped women achieve certain rights in some areas. For example, at work, women always had lower salaries compared to men, but now it is different, and women get the same salaries and benefits; I do believe women have the same salaries as men. At home, women have also attained some rights because now men share many things with their wives such as house chores and taking care of the children. Women have achieved many positions in politics, just like men; women have also had many accomplishments in sports. In general, I think women have reached many goals in society.

I think there are still more rights for men in areas like the workplace. Men are also allowed to be unfaithful in a sense, which I don't think is right. There are many professional women, now that women have the right to go to school, but it has also to do with what State women live in; for instance, women in Chiapas, Oaxaca, and Guerrero, who are peasants or earn a low income, don't have too many rights. They can't afford to go to school. I think that these peasant women don't have the same rights as men because their husbands don't have the capacity to understand and let their women go to school to study. I know that women who can go to college can decide to specialize in areas that used to be just for men, like medicine, engineering, and graphic design.

Women have sexual freedom – society does not condemn them like before. Now women have the right to live with their partners without getting married; they can live with them for two or three years before marriage, and they have the chance to decide if they want to marry them or not. Women enjoy this kind of freedom now and society doesn't look down at them. I think it is different now than it was before.

I think women do receive the same salary as men, but I think there is still a lot of machismo in society, and it depends on the company, too. I guess it should be that women get the same salary for the same job, but I don't know exactly. In some corporations women make the same salary and not in others – I think it depends on the place where they work. It depends on the company's owners and managers.

In my times women had to follow the roles that society imposed on them, but these days there is more freedom. Now women have more freedom to follow a professional career, and they don't stop their professional jobs. However, women also have to take care of their families; my daughter, for instance, has a good professional job, but she takes care of her kids at home, too. These days the roles for women are not as marked as before – now, women and men share more responsibilities, like raising kids together. I guess 20 years ago society was stricter on women's roles.

I know feminist writers like Angeles Mastretta, Guadalupe Loaeza, and Carmen Aristegui. They talk and write about women and support their rights. They influence other women through their books and their actions; because of that, other women become conscious of their rights.

My education at home was very traditional; you learned that you had to be married as a virgin, to take care of your home, your husband, and your kids – that is the way our parents taught us. I didn't learn that I could have the same rights as men. Men were men and women had to be dedicated to their homes. If you happened to have a college education, sometimes you had to quit your professional job to take care of your home and raise your children.

My mother never talked to me about my sexuality. When the occasion presented itself, I discovered that she never mentioned anything about menstruation and never said anything about my wedding night at all. However, now I do agree that mothers should talk to their daughters about their sexuality. I did talk to my son and daughter about their sexuality – I talked to my son about masturbation and other sexual topics. I remember my mother used to tell us not to let anyone kiss us in the ears and not to let anyone touch our breasts (there is the belief in Mexican society that a man can arouse a girl by kissing her in the ears and neck). I never told my daughter that she had to be a virgin until she got married.

I think Mexican society is very patriarchal. Men are the head of the house. My husband always supported my professional career – he gave me my space, I could go out with my friends, and he helped me with our kids, but my husband was very upset when our daughter decided to go live on her own in her own apartment. He used to argue that she didn't have to do that because everything was provided for her at home.

We don't talk about women's rights at home – not now or when my kids were at home. We used to talk about the kids' school and other topics, but we never mentioned women's rights to them. Look, values are values, and I would like for future generations to follow the morals and values instilled in women by their parents. Good principles and values are important for a family. I'd like for women in the future to keep fighting for their rights and keep their values and morals, and I'd like for them to have the same rights as men.

Interview 4: Clara, 47 years old, housewife

Feminism is a social and historic movement that has taken place in many countries to improve conditions in every aspect of women's lives. I consider myself a feminist. I work every day and exercise my right to make my own decisions and to be a person with rights and responsibilities. That's the way I approach what I do. I don't know anything about the feminist movement that took place during the '70s and '80s in Mexico, but some of my family members, like my nieces and sisters, are part of groups that work with related themes and are women's rights activists.

I believe feminism has helped today's Mexican women achieve the same rights as men, although I don't believe feminism is enough. Nowadays, it is very noticeable that there is a better response towards abuse against women based on whether it is a woman or a man. I don't believe that women could have obtained more rights in society without feminism and other women that have fought for more rights. That would imply that these rights came about on their own because it was considered normal for women to have less rights or freedoms than men. However, it wasn't like this before, women having more rights than men, and I don't think that this would have changed just because.

All the rights that pertain to all humans are shared between men and women, even though unjust conditions remain, such as women earning less money or the sexism that remains present in some aspects of the workforce. Men prefer to work with men as equals, but they prefer women as subordinates. At least people can look forward to more rights for women in Mexico, but I know this is not the case in other countries.

There are more opportunities for academic preparation for women now than before because fathers wouldn't let their daughters study, or they considered school a useless waste of money – in the end, their daughters would get married and their husbands would support them financially if they remained married regardless of what happened. Now, more women can study and support themselves.

I believe women have sexual liberty that isn't tied to a marriage, even though there are still many prejudices, like the ones that have always existed. I don't believe women receive the same salary as men for working the same job in Mexico. Women regularly earn less money than men and have jobs at lower levels than them.

Both in small towns and cities there are still people that would think badly of a man washing dishes. It is expected that women be the ones to work in housekeeping or be in positions as receptionists or secretaries. However, there are also lots of women that prepare themselves and become doctors, administrators, and engineers. It's true that society creates a role for women, but women can also decide what to do or decide whether what is expected of them is important.

I don't know any Mexican authors that identify as feminists; therefore, I don't know how they influence awareness about the topic of women's rights. My parents always supported me a lot, and at home there were things my brothers did and things that women did. However, now they see us all as equals and hope that we are all happy.

My mother would talk to me about my sexuality when I was younger. I don't think it's a topic that should be prohibited or shameful. Mothers should give their daughters advice that they want and need. I believe that Mexican society is profoundly patriarchal. Many things are based on the leadership of a man – up until today, all our presidents have been men, and even when we think about politicians and powerful people that manage companies, they are largely men. My husband supports me in my daily and professional life – we work equally and support one another as much as possible in matters related to our home, our children, and our business.

When the topic arises, we talk about feminism at home. We can't omit some comments about how society works in terms of being a man or a woman. I'd like for future generations of women not to have to worry about being a woman, and instead worry about what they want to be. Prejudice based on gender is absurd and I'd like for that absurd way of looking at differences to end someday, and for us to be able to talk more about people instead of talking about men and women.

Interview 5: Silvia, 60 years old, housewife

Well, in the era that I am from, women were a bit disregarded. I think that, lately, there has been improvement, but women were disregarded and mistreated, particularly psychologically with the phrases "you cannot," "you don't know," and "you're not useful," which lower self-esteem. I think that even if a person's self-esteem was more or less okay, with that constant treatment, it could get lower. I believe that there has been improvement, but I have the impression that now we are going to the other side. I believe it is about seeking balance, right? That women aren't men and men aren't women. I've heard that now teenage girls have sex with many teenage boys, they have first dates, and I don't know what else. It can't be, because I believe women are more sentimental, right? But, in the end, that's my perspective of women from back then and women now.

My parents would never talk to me about my sexuality. Never. For me, it was just "be careful" and "take care of yourself." Well, yes, but be careful with what? What do I need to be careful with? I think that, if I were a cartoon, my eyes would look super huge. With what? I didn't even know what my dad was talking about. I never knew. In fact, like any other person, one starts to get curious and asks, "Why is that?" I remember that one of my curiosities was how babies are born, and it was an aunt that told me about it, but my mom would never. The topic was prohibited at home. My family wouldn't talk about it. I would have liked it if my mom talked to me about it more. I think what was happening is that she didn't have education, because she reacted the same way with religion; for example, I'd ask her, "Hey Mom, why does God do this?" And she would get angry and tell me, "Oh, stupid teenager, you don't know anything," and those were her responses. It would be worse for me because I would want to know, and she'd call me stupid and tell me that I didn't know. Well, of course I didn't know, and that's why I was asking, now it's clear, but back then it wasn't.

I have one daughter. She's an adult now, but when I finally wanted to talk to her about sex, she told me that they'd already explained it to her at school and that she already knew. With my sons – I've also spoken with my son since high school, and I've told him that he has to use protection, and I still, well, not now because he's a lot older, but I told him that one day he would love a woman very much and he might [make her sick, get her pregnant], all for a moment of passion.

I adjusted myself to the times regarding this topic. In fact, I also spoke with my daughter since high school, it's the truth. It was harder with her because I was her mother, and I wanted to talk to her but I also didn't because I didn't know much, right? I was ashamed of how to start the dialogue, but bit by bit I started to tell her and she, very naturally, responded, "They've already told me at school." In a way, it helped. I no longer feel constricted when we discuss these topics. I'm from a small town and, for example, I notice that my cousins over there do feel very closed off. They're a lot more closed off and I think that maybe it's the fact that I live in a city, that I listen, or that I have means of communication.

I don't believe that society punishes or represses women for their sexual liberty or their habits. In fact, I was a single mother, and I believe that when I became a mother – my daughter is 40 years old now – when I was a single mother, I think it was a bit pointed at, but not as much as before, because, well, in my case, I had a sexual relationship with someone and I wanted a record that I was, in my mind, in love with that person, but there were always people that told me to act smart. I thought, "Well, it's not that I'm stupid, I wanted a child." Maybe I didn't know how to measure the consequences and the responsibilities that would come with it, but I knew that I wanted a child. It was very bothersome, especially when people that I didn't even acknowledge in my daily life would give me their opinions. Right now, I believe that women have support, and I'm very thankful for my mother because she supported me in my decision. She supported me every step of the way.

It's very clear for me now that someone in that fragile state of mind, with no support, could end up anywhere because of the disorientation, right? The weight of the world is on your shoulders and you think, "How do I support this child?" I'm not saying that this is the case for everyone, but it is for some women. Long ago, it was very much frowned upon, simply the idea of having a child without being married. The child would suffer the consequences, the mother was insignificant, even if she'd only been with that one man. Hearing about women who were murdered by their parents because of a pregnancy, it was like a horror novel. I learned about those cases. You're supposed to love and support your children more than anything.

I had three younger brothers and sisters. My father died when I was 12. He was sick for a long time. He died at 35 years old. He'd emphasize the idea that people had to know their worth because they were people. My father would talk to us a lot about, well, at the time, for him, it was important that we didn't get involved with men like that, without getting married. He told us that we were worthwhile, and because of that we had to demand respect. He'd tell us a lot that we deserved respect, but it was the same thing. Because of my age, I thought, "What are you talking about?" I was very young. I didn't have the knowledge to see more. It wasn't clear to me.

In my family my mother would highlight the differences between men and women. It's understood that men are worth a bit more, that they have more value. In fact, to this day, I have two sons and a sister that has sons. She feels like she has to cater to men more, but I don't. It's weird, but I don't feel that way. In fact, my mother-in-law took care of my sons for some years, when they were little, and she would tell my son, "Stand up, like this, and they'll dress you." I'd tell him, "No, it can't be like that. You can dress yourself." She had that mentality that men exist to be served.

What happened is that my youngest son had a stroke and I had to stop working. I felt very happy at work. I don't think it makes sense to stay home all day, knitting napkins, and taking care of the family. I feel very satisfied when I am able to work because I feel that people recognize that. Well, I was also lucky enough to work with men that valued me as a woman because one of the men that I worked with told the workers at the warehouse, "She's here because I want her here and you have to obey her." It was very important, and they'd tell me, "I need you to be more aggressive."

I've heard that society is still like that, that men get priority or preferential treatment at work. Personally, I never experienced that. I had two other transitory jobs, transitory because they lasted less than a year. Before my son fell ill, I worked at a place that had tons of drivers and experienced the same things.

My husband hasn't put obstacles in the way of my studies, we're both studying, but it would cause problems if I studied by myself because he wouldn't understand why. My husband is very kind, but I perceive him as a bit machista. I mean, for some time, I did believe, "men are so dumb when it comes to being in charge." I do perceive it as a bit machista.

My husband is not violent or excessively machista. Sometimes yes, but one learns to be more mindful. I lived through a lot of violence, in my case, lots of violence during my childhood. I learned how to be mindful. I learned that it was better to shut up before provoking another incident. In fact, before my son got sick, we were going to separate. I stayed in the relationship, as did he, because of my son, who suffered from a hemorrhage. There are details that sometimes you're not willing to repeat.

I've asked my husband if he experienced violence during his childhood and he says he didn't, but I do talk about this with my son because he denies it. He has told me, and he is modern in that regard, he says that there are feminists that exaggerate, feminists that feel offended because people offer them seats on the bus or feel offended because people let them walk in front of them. They want equality. Given the era that I'm from, I find that exaggerated because it feels good when people pay attention to you. I mean, as a woman, I think it's fine and I'm thankful for it. If someone gives me his or her hand so I can get off the bus, I say "thank you." However, my son says that feminists exaggerate a lot. He told me, "You're a feminist." I responded, "Yes, I am. If you get married one day and mistreat your wife, I'll intervene. Be sure about that because here, a relationship either works or it doesn't, and, if it doesn't work, everyone goes his or her own way. I don't agree with you mistreating a girl." That already happened to my youngest brother, and even with the second-to-last one. They got married at 17 years old and, for reasons that people never found out about, he would beat her. I felt moved and intervened. I told him, "No, no, why are you hitting her? No, no . . . don't beat her." I was very blunt, as if she were my sister. If I could defend women and work in a place that provides support for abused women, I would do it happily because, many times, men abuse their physical strength and, sometimes, women forget their role and start to yell at men and make them violent. I say that because of my husband because when we got married, when we were newlyweds, we would fight, and he would turn around and leave and I would get very upset. I felt that if I had the physical strength, I would bring him back, but I couldn't really do that. I mean, he would have time outside and it was the best option, he'd come back, and I would be calmer. This is part of my history of violence.

The violence that I mention, the violence from my home, was due to my parents. Maybe it's pointless, but my mom was a very pretty woman. At the time, if a woman was not a virgin when she got married, it was very frowned upon. So, my father would hit my mother, and my father's family thought that my mother wasn't a virgin when she got married. My mom was a very feisty woman, and would ask, "Why are you hitting me?" Maybe it's a part of why I am a feminist, seeing that she . . . despite everything, she didn't let it happen to her. She just didn't understand, and according to him, he would hit her because people would say that she was the boss of him. They would tell him that my mother bossed him around, and he would hit her to demonstrate that she wasn't in charge. That violence took place only with my mother. When my father would hit us, it would be because of my brother. He didn't have that violence that he had with my mother with us. He would hit us, though, spank us if we misbehaved.

I didn't hear about any feminist movements in Mexico during the '70s and '80s. I admire it. I just don't agree with women going to the other extreme. That would be, for example, women that want to scream at men. I believe that if the woman is the one that works and earns money and the man stays home to take care of the kids and manage the household, I don't see anything wrong with that because that's their agreement. I don't consider him less of a man. They're simply living in an affordable manner. I mean, whether or not the woman yells at the man. I have had to hear this, though. I live in an apartment and I have had to hear women who yell a lot at their men. What are they thinking? I mean, he's honest. That's what I mean when I refer to going to the other extreme. Men seem to take it, they take it until they get to a point, I believe, that they hit you.

That's not okay, it happens when the situation gets to the other extreme. Women shouldn't take advantage of people. I believe the most important thing in a relationship is respect, to be treated like a person because, just like how I respect you as a woman, you should also respect me as a man. I don't believe there are specific roles defined for men and women. I mean, as long as the husband keeps evolving, that's what I'm saying. If there's a successful, professional woman that gets married . . . in fact, I had a cousin like that. She was married to a deliveryman. She earned all of the money, and I didn't think that was bad. However, my uncles would call him a "wimp." Life brought them together like that. Why is it wrong?

I think, as a woman, I think we have so much to give because life gives us experience. Our experience is something that we can give our daughters in the future. I say this for myself because I've lived it. For example, when I was orphaned, I met a woman that wanted to teach me how to paint. It didn't take because I wasn't very creative, or it wasn't my time, I don't know, but I did go to make-up classes and I know how to apply make-up. I was about 13 or 14 years old then; some years passed, and my daughter was born, so almost 50 years passed. Maybe 40. One day, my daughter was very agitated. She told me, very upset, "It's that you're not doing my make-up! You don't know how to do make-up!" The fact of the matter is that I took it as a given and saw that I knew how to do make-up. That's what I'm saying, each person comes across situations that we're going to have lessons for. It would be so beautiful, for one to transmit, to really have that dedication, there are people that do make-up.

I'd like to keep asking women to study, now that I've been able to return to my studies. In fact, I've had to ask people who don't study, "Why are you wasting your time there?" I simply know that, for example, maybe I'll never study the profession that you all have, but it has been a gift for me because I'd still be watching the soap opera *La rosa de Guadalupe*. That's fine, but the point is to widen your horizon. There are other things that are worth enjoying. When I stopped working, I had more time to watch television. I have missed so much by watching those things that part of it starts to transform your mindset. It's not wrong to watch a short telenovela or read every once in a while.

No feminist novels come to mind when I think about whether or not I've read one. The fact that people say that that was the period in which Mexico had more development, it can't be. At that time, even if a woman had the support of a man, she's the one they'd point to. I think that there must be something, tons of women that have had many stories but, unfortunately there weren't many means of communication.

It's a gift because I believe life starts to end when we don't have anything to do, when we don't want to learn, and we can. For example, someone with limited income and nobody to orient her in the right direction, you could say that they're excused, but if the opportunity is there . . . it's a gift.

Interview 6: Obdulia, 50 years old, house cleaner

Feminism? I have heard stuff on the radio or on the news about femicide [*sic*] when they kill women. That they killed so-and-so. Actually, two months ago they were talking about a girl that complained that her husband beat her, and they did not do anything, so he killed her. He waited for her to leave her house, drop off her son, and he took her life. That is what I heard.

I think one of my daughters – the oldest – has suffered from that type of problem. But, as a woman, I think they go through this because they want to. Maybe you can stand the first blow, but not the second. Stop them, tell them, "You know what? This ends here." We have to respect ourselves as women, love ourselves. If you do not love yourself, or respect yourself, who is going to respect you? She tells me, "Well, I would go and complain." It is not about complaining, it is about you putting a halt to his behavior so that he stops messing with you.

Why do they not treat women and men equally if we can be equal? Maybe we can overcome this a bit. For example, women can work now. Women have their professions. They could not work before. Before, they had to be home. How many children did they have before? Up to 15 or 20 children because it was the only thing they could do. Have and raise children, nothing else.

I think it is great that women have the opportunity to get ahead, to be more than housewives. It is very good. I just do not like that women try to be more than men and humiliate them, and unfortunately, I had to live that episode. Exactly like a competition. As a woman, I do not like that. It is great that all of the women that are moving ahead have the opportunity to do so because they have bachelor's degrees and earn good money at their companies. That is good. It is great. I know that it is the man's obligation to support his family, but it is not 100% his obligation. A man cannot do it alone. If he supports you financially, you should maintain the household. Especially in this day and age. That is how people supported each other. I did not have to do that. I did not have to say, "No, my husband can support me."

I do not think people show respect, because now I see it in my family with my grandchildren. Back then, they would not let kids go to their partner's house. Now, they are even allowed to go in their bedrooms. "We are not doing anything!" But what are you doing then? It is a lack of respect. I tell my daughters, "Maybe I am a bit old fashioned, or very much so, but I do not think that is okay." Maybe I am too old fashioned, but I do not like that. They are in the house for a while, an hour or two. What can you talk to your girlfriend about for so long? They get there at five or six in the evening and leave at ten or eleven at night. I do not like it, but they are their children.

I left home at 15 years old. I got pregnant. You will not believe me, but I thought they would take my baby out through my stomach. I was never told where babies are born from. During my first menstruation I was never told anything. When I say "my parents," I mean my mother, because I did not have a father. I never met him. She is not here to confirm it, but maybe I, or my brother and I, because there are two of us, were the result of rape.

In my family, according to my grandmother, she had her daughter. She had three children, but two passed away and only my mom survived. My grandmother had to work, because she had no husband, and she would leave my mother alone. She would not leave her with food or anything. Apparently, according to what my grandmother would say, she found her one day, and she had eaten her own feces. That feces that she ate affected her brain, because she could not speak well. She was not dumb or slow, like they say. She was somewhat normal, but I think they raped her when she was really young. Really young, maybe 12 or 13 years old. But then she did not know anything else. My brother was born, and the man kept abusing my mom, I do not know. Her life was very, very sad.

I remember that she would get beaten. You would never know what was happening until my grandmother took her from that man one day. She picked us up, my mother and I, and took us to her house. I remember a little, my mother was beaten, indeed.

Sometimes parents force you to run away. They force you to leave home. I remember that my grandmother would have me working, I would wake up at six in the morning, and she would send me to work with a woman that sold "menudo." I would go out with her, but I was young. Then, I would leave that place and go with a lady that sold tostadas and clean there. I think that is why I like washing dishes. I was about five years old. I had a bench so that I could reach the dishes, at five years old.

People have sex now to see what it feels like. That is not alright with me. You should wait. Obviously, I know that girls know about sex as teenagers nowadays, but they should learn how to take care of themselves in school. As long as they take care of themselves, they can experience all of this later. There is an appropriate age for everything. I mean, for example, I made the mistake of leaving home, but there is so much freedom now. I did not have freedom. I am not saying this to defend myself or to say that it was okay. Maybe it was not okay.

When my daughter asked for permission to be with her boyfriend, it only lasted about three months. You feel embarrassed about it. "Oh, no, leave him because it is not convenient anymore." I told her, "no." She had to decide whether or not to leave her boyfriend. I asked her whether his parents knew about the situation. Now, the woman that gets pregnant, it is because she wants to, not because she does not know.

In my time, we really did not know what was going on about sex. We were very ignorant. Maybe it was just my family. Maybe there were families that told their children, I do not know. Like your mother, maybe she told her children, I do not know. My family never spoke of such things. It is bad because you feel dumb when you do not know what is going on, even about having children. The problem was that, I remember, they would talk about you if you were pregnant.

I did not speak to my daughters about this. I only spoke to them about their menstrual cycle, but on the topic of sex, I told them to be careful when they started menstruating. When a woman starts her cycle and she has intercourse with a man, she can get pregnant. I never told them, "Buy this, protect yourself." I only told them to be careful. It could be embarrassing. Even just going to the store to buy a feminine pad could be embarrassing. That is not the case now. Women even send men to buy them. I mean, it is okay now. Lots of men, not all of them, I see have changed their children's diapers when they urinate or defecate. That is hopeful, seeing men change diapers in this day and age. That is good. I think it is great, but there are women that take it too far. There should be a balance. It is alright for us to be equals, but there are a lot of women that take advantage of men. I saw my son yesterday, and he said, "Look how I have my hands because your daughter-in-law makes me do chores." "It is okay, son. You have to help your wife, too." I mean, just imagine it, she is falling apart. She washes clothes by hand, she has to cook, she has to take care of their daughter, and she just wants help. I do not want to say, "Oh, no, that is her responsibility because she is the woman." No, but she should not take advantage of him. I say that because there are other women that are abusive, saying, "Well, it is your turn" while they watch television. If both of them work, go ahead. You have to help each other because both of you work, but if she does not work and she wants her husband to wait on her, no. How do you see that?

My husband doesn't mind that I still work, so much so that he does not even know where I work. Really. He does not know where I work or who my bosses are. He never tried to psychoanalyze me. He does not mind if I talk on the phone, he never calls me to talk to me. I am okay with that. "Where are you? Where have you been?" He sees his friends, and sometimes men ask him, "Why is your wife working? What is wrong with her? She will cheat on you. If she stays home, she cannot cheat." He tells them, "No, if she wanted to do it, she would even do it at home. If she goes to the store, there are men there, too. There are men everywhere she goes. If she stays home, the plumber or the electrician show up." He is not like that. He is not machista. The only thing he says is that a married woman has no reason to talk to men. That is his only concern. It is the only machismo that he has, that married women have no reason to go out with friends.

I think it is important to teach daughters not to be submissive to men. My daughters are not like that, but their children talk back to them. It makes me sad because my children were not like that with me. They never talked back to me. The oldest one, who is 28 years old, I tell her about it, and I bring it to her attention, but she never talks back to me. Her kids say, "why are you butting in, mom? It is my life." What a spoiled child. That is what is wrong with my daughters.

My daughters work. The oldest one has a daughter, too. She worked while she was home. When she left with her boyfriend, she never worked again. He will not let her. She has whatever he gives her. They have a house because his grandmother gave them one, but she does not work. My other daughter, Isabel, she works, and she has kids. Unfortunately, they work because their husbands are not completely invested. Nowadays, women want to work because it lets you have more than what your husband gives you. If you want to buy something, they only give you enough for food or things for your children, but how can you buy things for yourself? Women that work can buy themselves whatever they want. If you want to buy another cell phone, you do not have to beg your husband. It is unpleasant to depend on your husband. It is unpleasant when you are young, but when you are older, it does not matter. You have already enjoyed life, and you had fun. At that point, if your husband supports you, that is okay.

When I was 15, I would say "I wish my husband supported me," but no. Now, we do not pay rent because we live with my sister-in-law, but we have to pay the electric bill and the water bill. It is okay for women to free themselves. If they want to be more than men, I am not sure. How are you going to be more than God? God is a man. How are you going to be equal to Him? I mean, it is good that women are not submissive. If you are going out with your friends, then go out together, but if they are not going then you should not go. Stay home. I told my daughters, if they do not want to be with their husbands, they can separate. If they like someone else, go ahead, but they have to be separated. The idea of leaving with a random man, if they cheat on you, it is because something is not working or because they are not happy.

The woman that was my daughter-in-law was manipulative. When she and my son separated, she hurt herself and then accused my son, saying that he hit her. I do not know what she was thinking. She did not lose the claim, I don't know why, but he, in the moment that they fought, he left her there and went to work. That is what she said, that he hit her, and he was working. But how did he hit her? Were there witnesses supporting what she was saying, that he hit her?

Interview 7: Sara, 54 years old, business owner

Feminism in Mexico? I think everything is bad. They say there is a lot of help for women but there is really nothing, it is too much talk and nothing else. For instance, they say that if a woman is beaten, she can go to the authorities to denounce a case, but they don't do anything. The authorities don't pay attention to what is going on. For feminism I understand that we are equal to men, but in reality, no one pays attention to women. Yes, I think Mexican society discriminates against us, women, but in fact we are more than men, we can do things better than them, and it is proven. For example, with my own kids, I was separated from my husband for four years and I am sure I did very well, better than him.

I don't remember any feminist movement in Mexico in the 1970s or 1980s, nothing. I do remember something about women who wanted equality with men, but I don't know when that was. No, I don't know of or have heard of any women fighting for equal rights, never.

Yes, I think Mexican feminism has had an impact in favor of women. For instance, in politics, I see women who are Representatives or Senators, that's where I see equality. With the new elections this year now there will be more women in politics with the new president Lopez Obrador. This is, I think, an advancement for women. I also think that there are more opportunities now for women to attend university. Many mothers and other women work, something that they couldn't do before. There are schools for women, too. I think all these changes would have happened with or without women fighting for rights; but I think that men wouldn't have agreed with these changes. Men want to see women down, without any rights and advancements in their lives. The worst that could happen to a man is to see a woman succeed. Yes, I think all these benefits were achieved by women, only by women.

I don't think men and women share the same rights and responsibilities. Very few men help their partners with their kids' upbringing or the house chores. Women are still the ones who work harder and more at home. I can count with my hands the men who would be willing to get home and cook for the family. They don't do it.

I think these days you see more things about women's sexuality. It was different before when there was more social criticism. Even in the way women dressed, now there is no judgment. Now women can enjoy more of a sexual relationship, and no one criticizes them. There is more freedom for women in many aspects.

I feel like there is still a lot of salary discrimination in Mexico. Even when women do more than men, they don't make the same money.

My education at home was a traditional one, my parents always told me to be a good girl, to get married, to be respected. We, the girls, didn't go out to parties, my sisters and me. If we wanted to go to a party we could go with my brother, that was the only way. I never had the same rights as my brother, not even for being the youngest kid in the family. For being the youngest I had to take care of my mother when she was sick; yes, my parents were very traditional with us.

No, my mother never talked to me about my own sexuality – she wouldn't even think about talking to me about it. I remember that when I talked to my mother about menstruation, because they had talked to us about it in school, she slapped me in the face because I wasn't supposed to know about it. I was about 11 or 12 years old when the teacher told us in elementary school. No, you should not know about that, is what my mother told me. Yes, I think nowadays mothers should talk to their daughters about sexuality. There are little girls having babies and they don't know anything. That is scary. It is a dangerous situation for both mothers and babies. I remember when my son was in secondary school, there was a pregnant girl who was 13 or something years old. What would she know?

Yes, I always talked to my kids about sexuality. For instance, I told my daughter not to let anyone touch her anywhere, nothing like someone asking her to let see her underwear or anything like that. Contrary to my own mother, I did talk to my daughter about menstruation and told her what was going to happen to her and her body and that she had to be very careful because she could get pregnant.

Yes, I think Mexican society is very macho. In specific the way men treat women. For instance, I told my daughter that once she had a kid, she would lose everything, but a man is still a man no matter what, men don't lose anything. We see macho men everywhere, low-lives who mistreat their women and their kids. My husband supports me in all my activities, but he still has some little macho characteristics. No one is free of those things. He used to control me by asking where I was, what I was doing. He wanted to keep a close eye on me.

I feel like people talk more about women's rights these days, but no, we never mentioned this topic in my house with my kids or in the family. Fortunately, my daughter is fine, she is married, and everything is just good for her. No, I don't think religion has anything to do with how women behave now. They don't care. It seems like religion has no value for many women. It was different back in my time when my parents took us to church every Sunday. My mother used to tell me to behave well, or that God was going to punish me.

I hope women these days will teach their daughters to behave well in the future, so they will be looked favorably upon by society and that they will fight for their rights. Well, yes, I might be a feminist since I always tell my female friends who had a hard life to fight for their rights. I tell them not to depend on their husbands for everything. And I tell them those things because sometimes they don't do anything that would make their husbands angry. I have told them that they have rights, to get a job, to do something for themselves. I wish my friends would be more independent and not to depend on what their husbands say, to fight for something for themselves. I think that I have changed, I am not like my mother used to be back in her time.

Interview 8: Goretti Alcalde, 70 years old, administrator of medical insurance for low-income families

I have heard a lot about feminism, as one word, one concept, with many meanings. There are those who take feminism as total freedom, but I don't consider it like that. There are those who take feminism as, how can I say it, an excuse to take advantage of it, which I don't think is healthy, and another meaning of a lot of licentiousness, which goes beyond any kind of good upbringing or morals, because it violates the rights of others, family, society, and it destroys everything.

No, I have never followed any feminist movement but there have been many. From the first ones, to get the same equality with men, and I don't agree with this, because to start with, we are not the same as men. I think the fight was about more rights for women. There is respect for those women's rights, but I think we, as women, have destroyed them because of social, political, cultural, religious conveniences. In the end that's what moved us, our personal conveniences according to our own environment in which we live, not our individual essence. It is more profitable to adapt myself to something than to fight for something else.

I have had different jobs throughout my life, and there has always been some discrimination against women. They say, for instance, "She can't do it because she is a woman, she won't be as productive because she might get pregnant at any moment, she will have kids and that is going to take time away from work." After some years a man can get hired working for a private or public company but for a woman who spent years raising her family that is not an option. It is something very subtle. They discriminate against women, and I went through that several times with friends and family. They don't hire you. It might not be as before, but it still happens.

Yes, there is a big difference to what used to be before to what happens today in terms of women's sexual activities, and I think it is wrong. This is a very personal topic and one acts according to what is our essence, our values, and principles. I don't like it and don't agree with it. Girls just don't get the same kind of upbringing as before, they are educated as boys and that's wrong, we are not the same. You are a boy, you are a boy, you are a girl then you are a girl. As a boy you have your advantages and limitations, and the same as a girl. So, we must define everyone's role in society, women can do as many activities as men, with some extra effort, but it is not about activities, it is about roles. Now we see that women want to take on the masculine role and we also see a lot of times that men want to take on the feminine role. There is nothing wrong with a man cooking meals, sweeping, or mopping, or doing all the chores at home, but in his role as a man, not to "wear a costume" as a woman. And vice versa, a woman doesn't have to pretend to be a man or act like a macho. I think that as parents and teachers, we must tell them what their role is for boys and girls, they don't have an identity and that's why some of them "wear a mask" that is more convenient to them, because they don't know since they were little kids what their roles are.

When I was a kid, education at home was very radical, we didn't have too many options. Black was black, and white was white, you are a man then you are a man, you are a woman, then you are a woman. Everyone had to do things according to their gender. If you want to study you will, and you will work and take care of yourself, but within your role as a woman. I was raised to follow certain roles. A man wears pants, a shirt, and no earrings or accessories, and that's what I like; earrings are for women, long hair is for women, short hair is for men. I understand how education at home works these days, but I don't think it is better than what I had.

Sex education at home was a taboo, and in that sense I think there have been some advances. But I think there is something wrong going on, too. In my days there were single mothers, but they were older, now it is impressive and alarming to see little 13- or 14-year-old pregnant girls. Their parents allow them to have boyfriends at an early age, that is not right, I was taught in a different way, and I did the same with my children. My upbringing was very traditional, but with my children I was more relaxed. They had the same rights and obligations. For instance, boys and girls shared all the chores at home: sweeping, mopping, washing dishes, cleaning bathrooms. Yes, a girl was a girl, but she was not the slave of the house or had to serve everyone, like back in my days when I had to serve my brothers.

I see a gloomy future for women. I see it to be very sad. In many circumstances women have passed the limits of feminism. By nature, we are stronger, and apparently all this evolution has been good, but it is distorted – we are not stopping. I can't imagine anything good for women, families, or society in the future. Women are the pillars, the supports that create harmony in the family, in society. Then, if we don't have moral strength in our minds, spirits, or education, what are we going to create? Nothing good. We must recover our identities as women, women's activities for women, without losing our roles. There are many police women, fire fighter women, but they are women who have not lost their identities as women within activities for men.

Interview 9: Lupita, 58 years old, house cleaner

Feminism is the – I don't know how to explain it – it is the, like, what they say, that women are the weak gender, it is like some people say that women can't do as much as men. But that is not true, women can do not only the same things as men but many more than people think. Feminism is the idea that we are stronger than men in some cases, obviously not in physical strength for instance. But in terms of intellectual capacity we can do things equally or better than men. Yes, based on what I just said, I think of myself as a feminist. I may have heard something about the feminist movement of the 1970s or 1980s but I don't remember paying any attention, so I can't talk about it. I personally don't know any women involved in the fight for women's rights, but I have heard of some of them on TV; I don't have any recollection of names. But there are women in politics, for instance the Peace Nobel Peace Price that was given to this lady, Rigoberta Menchu I think. I don't remember any names, but I do know that some women have done a lot of work on behalf of women's rights.

Yes, I think feminism has done a lot for women; for instance, like many years ago women didn't have the right to vote. Thanks to all the social movement around this, I don't know how, who or when, but women obtained the right to vote. More recently women have the right to earn the same salary as men for the same job, because men used to make more than women. So yes, I agree that women have gained more rights nowadays. Yes, men still have more rights than women, but in some cases, people share the same rights and responsibilities. For instance, some couples share the house chores, the relationships with their kids, that's something that didn't happen before. Still there are many men who think like they did in the past and don't do anything.

It is the same for example, with education. There is more motivation for women to attend school and college, and in the past, based on comments that I have heard, it was preferably men [who were] the ones with the right to study. Women were not inspired to continue with their education. Now I have noticed some changes. Women are enthusiastic about careers that were exclusive for men years ago.

I don't think women have more sexual freedom. Society reproaches women more than men if they have sexual activity out of wedlock. Yes, I think women have always had sex before marriage, and society still doesn't take it well; it is always the same.

For what I know women still make less money than men for the same job. Men always make more money than women – but I don't know, that is something I haven't seen myself. Yes, I have heard that there are a lot of disparities in that regard. No, I don't think Mexican society still influences women to be submissive or selfless. Now women fight more for their rights. I don't know any artists, writers, or public figures who identify themselves as feminist; I haven't paid attention to that.

My upbringing was very traditional, being a woman in my family meant to serve the men in the house. Married women had to take care of the kids, wash clothes, clean the house. Throughout the years, however, for what I know, things have changed and there are different ideas. New couples talk about how things must be in the present, they don't do things like in the past, everything has been evolving. Now men take care of the house, watch the kids, and do things that they didn't do before.

No, my mother never talked to me about my own sexuality either. Because I was a kid or a teenager, I wasn't supposed to hear about those things. Those things are of no interest to you, they used to tell us. In my case I couldn't ask. That was like blocking us from learning. Yes, of course, I think mothers should talk to their daughters about their sexuality; even though my upbringing was different, I think my mother made a mistake. I don't have daughters, only three boys, but I have talked to them. I think that having a daughter would have been different as there is like more freedom to talk to a daughter than to a son. I don't think religion has a big influence on women to keep them submissive to men; I think that is something that has changed. I was never told that I had to behave like a girl or God would punish me.

Yes, Mexican society is very macho, still. Even though there are people talking about changes, there are still many macho men. In some families, for instance, men say that just because they are the husbands, they should make all the decisions. They tell their wives to be quiet because the husbands decide on any conflicts with the kids or anything else. My husband is not macho, I have a lot of freedom, and we try to find solutions to any situation together regarding the house or the family. We do it as equals. Yes, my husband and I share the same rights and responsibilities.

Yes, we have talked about women's rights at home. It is not a common topic but yes, we have mentioned it. I have two married sons and one single, and when we talk about this we tell them not to behave like machos, that they must give freedom to their wives and the same obligations and rights. I would like for women to teach their daughters in the future that they should have self-respect, and to motivate them to enjoy the same rights and obligations as men, to be free to do whatever they like without becoming licentious and to be strong; not to be so sensitive or submissive.

Interview 10: Claudia, 38 years old, housewife

Well, what I have heard about feminism is that it is women's liberation, women who are fighting for the same rights as men, or who are fighting for equality. But for me, for what I think, is that God created men and women, right? And each one has their own role; there are things that women can do and things that men can do, and things that women just can't do and well, we must accept that. I think that God created man for him to be perfect and

God created woman to follow her own role. I would have liked for my mom to spend more time at home, to do what I am doing now, to stay with her children, to share with them. But she wanted to work more maybe trying to be equal to my dad. She wanted to provide more for her family, and she did but by neglecting her family, which is more important. So, it is not like women can't do some things that men can do, but women should perform their role and be with their children.

No, I don't consider myself to be a feminist, I like what I do, I like to be with my children, to be attentive to their needs, their upbringing, to pay attention to them. Then, I think that a feminist woman is after something different; I think she wants to work and to provide for her family as the husband does and I don't think that would be for me because my priority is my kids.

I have heard of a feminist movement in the 1970s and 1980s in Mexico which was very strong, but I really don't know much about it. We didn't have access to television – my dad was a very rigid, jealous person about everything, so we didn't have access to media at home. Neither have I heard of women fighting for their rights in general, just what you watch on the news about women trying to be equal to men in certain things, that they are fighting for that.

Women have more equality than before with jobs, with some jobs I suppose. Presently women have more rights than before to go to school. It was very different in the past. My mom, for example, never had the chance to attend school. She was working since she was a little girl. Her dad, that is my grandfather, always had her working for my grandmom at home. My mom was focused on working in the house and in her free time cleaning houses for other people to provide money for the family, but she never had the chance to go to school. I don't think women and men have the same rights and responsibilities in Mexico. There is no balance, but somehow, I think it is different now, it is not the same as before. I think men still have more rights than women. I witnessed many things with my dad. For instance, he was very possessive and jealous, and I basically spent my childhood isolated. I did go to school, they let me, but I was isolated, I didn't know my family from my mom's side, I don't remember anyone.

These days women have more sexual freedom than before without getting married. That has become the norm in Mexico, that someone has a boyfriend and two or three days later a different one, not just a boyfriend but someone to go to bed with and then another, and another. When I was a little girl, I couldn't talk to anyone, no one. My dad was very strict and what I see now is like wow, I am surprised at everything. Society still judges women for having sex outside marriage, but it is becoming more normal every day. It is becoming normal that young girls have sexual partners.

Oh, yes, I think there is a huge difference between salaries for men and women. I know of a lady, for instance, who cleans houses for other people, and her salary is very small. In the companies that hire men to do the same, I don't think that they make the same money as women, I think they make more. There is a lot of salary discrimination against women.

I don't know of any women, or haven't heard of women who have fought for women's rights. All I know is what I heard in the news when I was a little older about women fighting for some rights, and trying to be equal to men, not only in terms of salary but in many other things.

My upbringing at home was very traditional – my parents never told me that I could do the same things as a man. My father was strict, very strict. So, I think that affected me and my sister, and it defines who I am now. In the same way, my mom never talked to me about my own sexuality. I remember that I used to talk to a neighbor, an old lady, and that this lady had a daughter who told me not to drink sodas because that was going to make me pee blood. And I said, really? And she said, yes, it is true, that's what could happen. And well, when I had my first menstruation, I remember it was the soda's fault. It was so bad to think that because of drinking soda I had my period. My mom never had that kind of communication with me or my sister, I think. Now, I remember those things and try not to do the same with my kids. I am always giving both my daughter and my sons information. I do think that moms should talk to their kids about their knowledge. Sometimes, we, mothers, believe that our kids already know about sex, but that is not true. We keep the information to ourselves instead of telling them. We are supposed to love our children, God made us the way we are, and we shouldn't hide it; we are human beings and we have the right to know.

Mexican society is very macho and patriarchal. I can see it everywhere, even in my family. In my mom's neighborhood, it is very evident. For instance, one can see a family walking down the street with the man always in the front, and the woman and children following behind. It looks like the man is more powerful, but it is lack of equality. I would like, for example, for them to be more equal. A man should give a woman respect and be more equal. But I don't think it is always the man's fault. But some women who don't respect themselves, I don't know, I feel like some women think they have no value. For instance, I am Mexican, right? I teach my kids that they must learn how to wash their clothes, dishes, to do chores around the house because nothing is going to happen to them if they do, they won't lose their manhood. So, they are going to grow up not being machos. So, men have always had the idea that they are better than women. It is, for instance, like my grandmother who used to iron my grandfather's underwear. She did everything for him, so why not teach boys to do it themselves?

At home we never talked about women's rights, we talked about respecting women. I have always taught my sons that they should respect their sister, that women must be respected. One should love and respect their mothers, grandmothers, sisters, cousins, all women. But, no, we have never touched the topic of women working as a man. There was a time when my oldest son was talking about his wife who wanted to work to make money, but not in order to replace what he earns. I think there is a reason why God made men the head of the house, for them to be the providers, not women.

Interview 11: Goretti Flores, 36 years old, communications

Yes, I have heard about feminism. I have never participated in groups of that nature because I consider feminism to be too extreme based on all the things I have heard, so I don't agree with the radical manner in which it is presented. But yes, I have heard of it. It is like the woman can do it all and does not need anything. So, I don't think my view is as radical. At least for myself, it is not that way. And I also believe, I have not dug deeper, but I believe that feminism was not born that way. I have not researched further back to where it came from or how it came about, but I don't agree with that radical side about being a feminist who doesn't need the man for anything. It is what I know.

I see it, women's role, with a big change, a big evolution regarding misogyny if I go to that perspective. In my family – not directly with my parents, but with my paternal grandfather – it was a very misogynistic environment, so I had the opportunity to see and learn how my aunts grew up completely subjugated. So, the woman was meant for marriage and meant to marry who the parents decided to marry them with, and if they felt like it. Because if they did not feel like it (marrying the daughters) they went to a convent or they would be single for life because they needed to care for the parents. They were trapped in a situation where they had no liberties to decide if they wanted to study, work, get married, or have kids. It had to be what their parents decided, and in the end my grandmother did not have the chance to give her opinion and say "No, let them do what they want." On the contrary, she was also subjugated, so I think there has been a big evolution in the activities of women. Because she has the opportunity to decide what she wants to do, whether it is to subjugate herself, or to not subjugate herself. It is like a big jump.

Yes, yes I do see an evolution. There are important changes where women have already taken key positions as directors of large companies. But not everything is so accepted, and they run into many obstacles where it is not so simple to first arrive there and to perform. Misogynistic culture begins to put women's capacities to the test as in "How can you, being a woman, make more than me, or how can you earn more money than me?" This misogynistic attitude still exists in some companies a lot, well, I won't say a lot because I don't know the statistics, but there are still many jobs where a woman earns less than a man in the same position. So, in the last two years I have been twice unemployed and have come across that situation where men earn more than me for the same job. And additionally, in the job interviews they consider your age. They emphasize it, and at that point I didn't have that consciousness, or the observation before as to why they emphasize my personal plans of "Why are you 36 years old and unmarried with no children?" And, if your plans are to marry and have children then that's it. I suppose that this is the side employers are aiming for, "If you're going to get married soon and have children, since you are 36 years old, then it isn't convenient for me to hire you right now." I do feel that it is this way. I don't know if that is why they really do it – I think so, because if not, they would ask it in the end, so it is like, really? Why are you discriminating against me because I am 36 years old? Even if there is that opening for women, why do they emphasize that part of the interview? At the end, when you get the position you realize that there is a man who started at the company at the same time as you, who earns more and maybe he has some other privileges. It could be.

You see, on the topic of discrimination, in that part, like I have just told you, that's the way it was at my last job. We started at the same time, one man and one woman and he made more than me. I became good friends with him, so we had all the confidence and openness to ask, "How much did they hire you for?" and we were doing the same thing in the same area, etc. He earned more than me. He earned 4,000–5,000 pesos ($210–260USD) per month more than me, so it was a very significant difference for the same job. On the other hand, I have suffered – well not suffered, let's say that it was a benefit – that because I was a woman on a team full of men, there was a type of coddling, of spoiling where they treated me like I was dumb, to pressure me to quit, but in the end, they didn't treat me as badly as they would have in a misogynistic culture, by saying "She is a woman, just leave her alone. It's okay we have to eliminate her." I felt that part, even if they were bothering me or setting me aside, not integrating me into new projects, advances, and conventions. So in those types of things the aggression or discrimination was not so direct, it was in some way like "Well let's coddle her because poor thing, she is a woman and she won't be of use, and in the end we'll remove her" and in the end they did fire me, and everything was peaceful. Not like in a misogynistic culture where I am going to give you a hard time. Not like that, I was able to navigate the situation quite comfortably, but in the end, it was also that part of me being the only woman.

You see, it is curious, my father was brought up in a misogynistic family, but he was not a misogynist. Sometimes he showed certain signs of it, but this was very slight. He controlled it well, and I remember a lot because for example, like I commented to you about how my grandmother was sub-jugated, my dad turned into my grandfather's polar opposite. They were opposite poles in the sense that my grandfather was very misogynistic and blatant about it, and my dad wasn't. My father integrated the women into the family, into sharing and sitting down to eat with them at the same time. My grandfather was not in agreement with this, but my dad was his polar opposite and he (my grandfather) respected his decision. My dad for exam-ple would take my grandmother, aunts, and me out together, but my father valued the women in his home. I grew up with that position of uniformity with my brothers because I am the only woman. I have two brothers and I grew up with that equality where "You can do the laundry, but you can too. You can fry an egg, but you as a man can as well. Your sister is not here to wash for you or cater to you at all." We were all the same. My mom still nagged us so that we all learned and respected our chores. She divided us and said, "You have to do this and that, and you get the clothes, you hang them, and you can fold them, now you have to dust, and you have to clean" like that. So it was very equal. I didn't grow up being bad or being less, rather, just like my brothers.

No, not there. Even though there was openness on that other side, for sex that theme was not touched upon. Also, in the part of books, during high school they talked to you about the menstrual cycle. The man changes, and so does the woman – those themes were not talked about at home. There was no chance with my mom or with my dad. With neither of them. And the time for example that I started my period I was already "old." I was the last of the high school girls to menstruate and I had not started. I had classmates who had already started their periods by the time they got to high school. But I never said anything at home. When I started, it was before I finished my third year of high school, are you kidding? I was 15 almost 16, so it was like "I already started." And my mom's answer was "You have to take good care of yourself." Grandmas and aunts would say that you couldn't eat lemon, you can't eat nopales, you can't eat this or that, a bunch of foolish-ness because I never had that chat with my mom and they were topics where she beat around the bush. As soon as I told her my mom would beat around the bush and I think that my dad would as well. Also, as a woman I wasn't going to ask my dad, right? So, it was curious because my dad is a veteri-narian, so the topic of sexuality in animals, reproduction in animals, isn't it very natural? The stallion is on top of the mare, the cow is giving birth. He saw those things as very natural. In the end I think that it helped me to say it's something very natural, but the topic was never touched on at home, and with TV programs at night with soap operas we saw the Telerín family. But if there was something we stayed up late for, it was for the soap operas where we could see them kissing, and my dad would say "Hey! Kids, go to bed! It's bed time!" We could not see people kiss on TV, but we did see our parents kiss and hug each other, but not on TV. In that time there were no remote controls, TV channels would be changed with a little device, a little knob. Now it amuses me, but at that time there was no chance for us to stay up (watching TV). Everyone had to go to bed. The topic was not touched upon. Although while inseminating the cows and the mares, he would put his hand inside of them. Are you kidding?

I think that there is still a conservative attitude. I'm not that open until I have a lot of trust with that person. Even if we had a lot of trust at home and in the family, the sex subject would not be touched upon. Now I can do it. Not right away, but with trust, I can talk about adventures or anything, right? Or questions and the rest. Jeez, you must have a lot of knowledge, but also an openness to speaking, asking, and guiding or searching for guidance. If I had a daughter, I consider that this would be very essential on my part in order to be able to help her, because right now young people – if I figured it out through textbooks, and only what was in the books, there was no other way, because it was a time when libraries were used, but there were not a lot of books where I could learn more things. Now on the internet, come on, there are explicit sex scenes or a sexual relationship, and not only that but also sick relationships, right? With animals, with dead people, with etc. etc. So, I consider that my stance is being more open and being able to talk about this with my peers, my children, not only women. Because they can find a lot of information that is not healthy, and they can learn in an unhealthy way.

I think that women can contribute, and they have contributed consciousness. Consciousness in that the woman has all the capacities to do something that the man can do as well. I don't know, it occurs to me right now: loading a water dispenser. A woman can do it, in a more careful way maybe because a woman's physical strength tends to be less than a man's, but it is just a matter of thought, or of knowing how to do things; maybe pushing it, rolling it, or dragging it. But she has the capacity to solve something that is labelled as being meant only for a man. So, I think yes, I believe that these feminist movements open the view on the capacities a woman has and about what she can achieve.

Regarding men, feminism gives a hard time to misogynists! It can be that they get a low self-esteem when they see themselves attacked, or it can be the other side where they get aggressive personalities and say, "No, you won't do better than me." Although there is also a positive side, where the man says "Oh, wow! You can also do this! So now I can also, as a man, do things that women do." Then we can see the scale becoming more equal.

I remember a woman who fought for women's rights. She was a nurse that participated in WWII with knowledge of aromatherapy, so she could sometimes do more things than a doctor. With her being a nurse and having a knowledge of herbology, essential oils, and things like that she was able to do more than the science of an intellectual man, giving service in WWII, but in a lesser degree since she was a nurse, a helper to the doctor. Yet she was able to create more results of physical healing.

What I think about feminists is that they don't have to be so extremist. It's important to have a balance between one thing and the other, and to not throw oneself into something without the proper information. I'm saying opinions, movements, whatever it is, but if you don't have a sustainable argument or an argument which is beneficial, it's better not to say anything if you don't bring something to the table. Don't just critique and point the finger, if you don't add anything beneficial, don't say anything. Don't start creating wars and going on marches if you are not contributing anything good. I think it should be – or well, maybe it's better for them to be so extreme, I don't know. But it is worth it to search for that balance.

Interview 12: Alejandra, 24 years old, revenue management for Aero México

Feminism is the fight for equal rights for men and women. That's just feminism. Yeah. That's what I believe that's how it started. Now it's getting like, different variations from feminism and there are people that think women are better than men.

I don't know, there are a lot of women that defend women by themselves, and think that they are superior to men, and they take that as feminism, or they just defend things that are not so defendable, and they see men as bad people, and they're against men. That's not feminism, that's like, hate, that's feminazi. But feminism itself should be, like, looking for the same rights for men and women. I do define myself as a feminist, because I know, and I expect to get the same opportunities as men. I know I can do things the same as a man, I know I'm good at things, I know I can achieve the same goals, or achieve any goal if I want to, and I don't believe a man can do things better than me – except for some things that are like – we are different biologically, so men are better in some things and women are better in some things, like naturally or physically. Like even in our mental structure we're different, so we would not achieve the same things in the same way. Men can probably achieve some things easier than women, because of how they think, and the other way around, but I don't believe a man has more chances of achieving anything than me. And, I know I can get the same opportunities and the same things. I don't believe I'm less than any guy.

I'm not really, like, I don't know much about the feminist movement of the 1970s and 1980s. I know it was a time when women started fighting for their own rights and that's it. I guess it was just like a social revolution, because women were not happy with their situation and how they managed their own lives. I think it has a lot to do with, well yeah, with development itself and it was something natural to happen, and that's it. I know they achieved a lot of things, and if they wouldn't have fought for our rights we wouldn't be in this situation.

Because feminism itself, it's a movement of women to change their current situation, and to change their opportunities and the way we culturally see women, but if this movement had never started, we would be in the same situation as the '70s or '80s, and we would have no different opportunities and different perspectives. Our cultural structure wouldn't have changed, nobody would have done anything about women and how we see women in our society. So I believe yes, our current situation is due to feminism and the constant fighting from certain women to get better opportunities, and to be seen differently by society and to be perceived as capable beings and not just what we used to be seen as.

No, I don't think it would have been the same, because as women, we limit ourselves a lot by society, so if society wouldn't have started changing and believing in women achieving more than being just in our homes and taking care of kids, no girl would have had the ambition, or would have the desire to achieve more than what society was expecting them to achieve. They would have never thought about doing some things differently or going out to undertake their own professional career or doing more than just staying home. So yes, I believe this movement has helped women to achieve bigger goals, yeah, higher goals each time, and to expect more of ourselves, not expecting to just be helped and then achieving their goals. It has helped a lot.

I believe it's much better now about women attending school. I don't think we have access to all the majors in college. It happened to me, personally. I wanted to study Economics, and they wouldn't let me at home because they said it was a male's major and they told me to study Psychology first and to be a psychologist or something easier. That's what they said. Something that didn't have so much math or anything. I was very mad. It was a strong fight in my home, for them to let me study engineering. Actually, in the end, I never told them what I was going to study, I just registered for a major, and I told them which university. I told them I was already registered for the major, but I never told them it was engineering until I started classes, because they wouldn't have approved it, and that's where the problem is. It's probably not because you can't attend university, or they won't accept you. It's cultural – our mental structure in our homes. They'll say we're not good at it, they'll say we won't make it, so in order to get to a major that's male dominated, you have to go through different obstacles, so it's really hard to get into a male-dominated major. Not because of the situation, not because they'll block you, but because mentally you end up quitting. You think "Okay yeah, I'll find something easier" or "I won't make it, they are right" but, yeah, so it is hard. It's like running a marathon. You're always thinking you won't be able to do it because everybody is telling you, you won't be able to do it. Because you're a woman. So, yes you can get into some major or male-dominated area, but it's hard. You're always fighting people and you're always fighting yourself, and trying to prove that you're good enough to do it.

In Mexico, I don't think we're free to have sexual relationships outside – not necessarily marriage but, like, a relationship. Because, you can do it, everybody will judge you and they will put certain stereotypes – they will put you in a certain stereotype. Men won't respect you because they'll say you're a whore and you are nothing more than that. I think you do lose a lot of respect for having sex without a formal relationship. People don't take you seriously, yeah – it feels like you lose value if you do that or you sleep with a lot of guys, and I think that's terrible. I don't think we are free in that aspect. Men are also judged, but differently, like the other way around, because if you are a male and you go out with a lot of girls, and you have sex with the hottest girl on the planet, then you're a winner, you're recognized. But if you're a girl and you go out, and even if you have an affair with the hottest guy, you're a whore.

In terms of salary discrimination, it's different from what I used to believe. I worked in AXA, that is a French company and they were very millennial, and they would take care of a lot of employees and promote equality and rights. It was a nice working environment with a lot of freedom, but I was completely aware that women earned less money than men, especially in higher positions and that was weird for me. Then I went to Aero México, which is a Mexican company, and I was expecting it to be more misogynistic than AXA, and in Aero México they earned the same, women and men; it's the same. And it's a super traditional company, so it was a weird thing, it's the opposite of what I was expecting. I would expect AXA to pay more – well to pay the same – and Aero México maybe to pay women less, but it was the other way around. And I believe professionally, all the women that are in higher positions, they have a strong personality. And you start, like, earning respect from men, but you have to earn it. It's really hard. I actually had this experience in AXA. There was a French director, and I had to work a lot with him. And when I first started working with him, if I found him in the elevator or on the walkways, he wouldn't even say hi until I started being strong in personality, and I started having certain kinds of success in my job. Then he started saying hi and he even told me I had earned it. So, why? Why wouldn't I deserve his respect unless I started achieving things, and he wouldn't do it with men? That's what made me really uncomfortable, and you realize that they assume you're not going to get anywhere because you're a girl. Or that you're not going to achieve anything, or that you won't have the required personality or the required strength to climb higher inside the company. So, you have to earn it a lot, and in the end your salary depends on how much you're worth for the company, and I believe as a woman, you're worth more if you show them that you're strong, you can maintain your opinion in front of men, and that you can defend it. I think that's a fight that men don't really have. Men have to achieve certain goals to get respect and get into higher positions, but they never have to demonstrate anything just for the sake of demonstrating it. As a woman you have to, and that's it. For example, in Aero México, there are many more women that are leaders than in AXA. In Aero México, my director is a woman, and my manager is a woman and they're strong, they're respected, and I feel like there are many more opportunities in Aero México for women than in AXA. Maybe it's the association with Delta because most of the directors are from Delta and they are all men. The VPs are always men.

Yes exactly, because they enjoy being right and telling you you're wrong, Mexico is very patriarchal. As a woman I have noticed it. I actually have even researched things for men in business to listen to you, and I once read a study that says as a woman in a meeting you have to speak 30% higher in your voice level than everyone else, or else they'll say no instantly, or they'll try to reject your argument as soon as possible. I'm referring to men especially, because I feel like they don't like being told what to do or how to do it, or they feel like if you tell them what to do and you're right, it's like telling them they are wrong. It's the ego thing we're always talking about, and they don't listen to you, and they fight in such an animal way. They don't care about what's right or wrong, they only care about their argument being right. And even if they realize they are wrong, and you are right, they won't accept it. At least not in a meeting or publicly.

So, you have to find strategic ways to guide men, but in the end, the recognition will never be yours because they always fight for the recognition. So, maybe you have to make a decision and you have to come to that decision with a man, and the man says, "A is the right answer" and you believe it's B. And if you want the final answer to be B you have to talk to the man and convince him to say B, but I will never win the argument if I fight with him thinking I have the right answer in a meeting for example – I will never win.

I have this experience. In my job, I have to work in pairs to achieve our goals and manage our markets; we have two different roles and we work together. I used to work with a girl and then they changed her and now I am working with a male. My manager, when we were changing to this guy, she talked to me and told me, "You have to be really strong and smart because he is a very dominant guy, and it's going to take a lot from you, and you cannot let him oppress you." And I had a lot of problems with him, and we didn't have good results at the beginning because everything – any strategy I would defend, he would say no, and he would tell me what to do – he would come and tell me how to do things. But, I should decide how to do things, because it's my job, and that pissed me off a lot because I can make those decisions, that's why they pay me. Why does he need to come and tell me what to do? And he would constantly do it, and we would have a lot of fights. Probably a month fighting and not getting to any results. It was quite hard, and then I started to do things to convince him of other things, but differently, but not by confronting him because if I confronted him he would say no.

I know certain women who have fought for their rights. I'm not sure if they are self-identified as feminists but for example, Elena Poniatowska. I believe she's a feminist because she has achieved a lot of things not only as a writer but politically. That for me, you don't have to identify yourself as a feminist to be a feminist. She's aiming for higher goals, and just believing in herself to achieve those things. Especially politically, that for me is feminism, and it's a motivation or inspiration for other women to do the same. That is providing feminism, it is providing equal rights and promoting equality in society. To tell women "you can look for something more than just traditional goals for women" and to tell everybody "women can also do this" – so I believe that's feminism.

My parents are divorced, and my father always raised me exactly like anyone else. He would always say – well, he would never even mention differences between women and men and he taught me to do everything by myself. For example, things that guys normally do. He gave me my car, he taught me to drive since I was really young, and he taught me how to take care of my own car, and things that are recognized as man stuff, and he always taught me to be self-sufficient and not dependent on anyone, especially on a man. He wouldn't even mention that. It was something natural for him that I would do those things, and I would be capable of taking care of myself, and anything I wanted, any goal I had. My mom, she's different. At the beginning she was like my dad, but then she got remarried and everything changed. I was told in my home to do certain things, to dress in special ways, and I remember especially, she started telling me how I should behave like a lady, as a nice family lady, like a family girl. It started creating a lot of conflicts in me. I had never thought in that way, but it was her husband's ideas, it was stereotyped, and she started teaching me to behave "right," to dress in a certain way, to take care of my appearance in certain ways. To not wear short clothes or to not show a lot and to behave well in front of men. Those kinds of things, which is completely different than what I had learned before and how my father was. So, I had two different points of view, and what I find the most interesting is that my mom changed so much after she remarried.

My mom did talk to me about sexuality. And I do believe it is something we should talk about with our daughters because in the end, it is your responsibility, it is your body, and you have to take care of yourself; nobody else will. Yes, she was always really helpful with that. She always supported me, was quite open, and she told me everything I needed to know. She helped me with all of my issues, she told me if I should take pills or if I should not take pills. She would get involved with it, and she would take care of me a lot. And my father also talked to me about it when I turned 18. He was also supportive. I guess it also has to do a lot with – well, my mom got pregnant really young, and they wouldn't want me to be in the same situation.

Yes. I think Mexico is a macho society, but I also think it's something natural. I'm going to talk about my ex-boyfriend because that's the only reference I have on this. He would do a lot of things for me. But also he had a lot of respect for my decisions. If I told him "I want to be the president of Mexico" he would say, "Okay, you are capable of doing it" and he would support me a lot, but in some other things he knew it was hard for me to do as a woman, simple stuff like taking my car to the mechanic. If I go the mechanic, they try to charge me a lot, or they won't respect me, or they will be looking at me in a disgusting way the whole time, but he would do that for me, not in a bad way. More in a natural way because that's how it really is, and well he made things easier for me, but I never felt like he was oppressing me. I do think our society is patriarchal because men normally take care of women, especially in marriage, and women expect men to take care of them, so I think it's a cultural agreement that we have, and nobody sees that as a bad thing to do.

Well, at home we don't talk about women's rights, we don't talk about it. It's something we see daily and that's it. My parents have their own beliefs. For example, my father, he won't ever talk to me about my rights as a woman or if I was a boy. He always starts from the agreement that I have all the rights. I don't have less or more rights than a male. But he doesn't really talk about it, he just tells me to do things or motivates me, he never says no to any of my goals, he never limits me, but that's just the difference. And in my mom's house, my sisters are dressing a certain way, and they behave in a certain way. They are girly, but if they want to do something, they do it. They are never told don't do it because you are a girl, but they do teach them to be a certain way, which I believe ends up in a certain kind of stereotype. For example, in my house, in the beginning, when we started living with my mom's husband, they were both working, and the decisions were made by the two of them. But as soon as my mom stopped working, the decisions were made by her husband and he would always have this argument that he would decide what to do because he was the one providing money for the house and that's terrible. The rights were not defined by male or female, but by who was providing the money, which is normally the male. And again, that's completely natural once you start having kids. It's biologically correct – well, not correct, the woman is the one taking care of the children and that's how we are made. We can't change that because it's something natural in women, and they have to be there and stop working. The problem is when you don't see this as being as valuable as making money for the house, and you as a person, and your decisions are more important than a woman because you are working and earning money. The role of the woman as a mother is also valuable. You cannot take the value away. That doesn't change how much their decision is worth.

What I would say to my daughters for the future? Just that you can achieve everything you want, you should never limit yourself, and that you always deserve the same respect as anyone else, as a boy or as a girl, your decisions. You have to be respected independently for how you think, your decisions, what you do, or how you behave in society and that's it.

Interview 13: Adriana, 74 years old, retired architect and languages teacher

From my own perspective, feminism is for women to have the same rights as men and the same salary; I think things have improved a lot from my generation to my daughter's generation. Look, since I don't know very well what feminism is about, I don't think I am a feminist because in my personal experience I never had problems for being a woman, I always received the same salary as my male coworkers, so I never had any problems, and I don't consider myself a feminist.

I don't remember any feminist movement in the 1970s or 1980s. I do know some feminist organizations now, which are of my daughter's generation, because she belongs to one of those organizations. However, I have some friends from my time who are very feminist, very radical. At some levels, I think feminism has helped women achieve some rights. At the professional level, for example, my daughter, in general, has a better salary than my son because, in part, she works for a foreign company and they offer good salaries, and the treatment they (the employees) receive is also better.

I think so, many of the rights that women have now are because other women before them fought to obtain those rights. Now, within the middle and upper-middle classes, men participate more doing chores at home, more women work outside the house and men must help – either with the kids' education or with taking care of them. It is very different from when I was young, very different.

Yes, women have more options to choose from in terms of college. Back in my time I was one of two women in architecture, I think that now 50% are women. No, sexual freedom in my time didn't exist, now it is different, very different – I can see it with my own daughter and her friends, it is totally different.

Maybe at some levels women have the same salary as men, but not in others. Perhaps foreign companies pay the same salaries, but not domestic companies or small ones, they just don't do it, especially family-owned companies where men usually make more money than women. In government agencies and offices men also make more than women.

It depends on the social class; I think that women in the middle and lower-middle classes must work both outside of the house and in the house following the traditional roles imposed by society, such as taking care of the children. For upper-middle class and above, I think that there is a balance between men and women; I can see it with my son and daughter who have the same roles at home with their spouses.

There are many women writers who identify themselves as feminist, but I don't remember their names – one of them is Guadalupe Loaeza. I think these women have a strong positive influence in society on both women and men. My parents were very open, especially my father, because he studied abroad, in Germany. Since I was a little girl, I knew that I was going to finish high school and that I was going to attend college. I could go out with my brothers, to parties, for instance. Other women from my time wouldn't be able to go to parties because their parents wouldn't let them go out. Yes, I was taught that I could enjoy the same freedom as any man.

My mother never talked to me about sex or my own sexuality. Now, my 11-year-old granddaughter knows everything from school. Mothers should talk to their daughters about their sexuality. I see, for instance, that my daughter talks to my granddaughter about those issues and I totally agree. In my times that wouldn't happen.

Mexican society is very patriarchal. It is less now than before. When I was young it was very patriarchal. For instance, marriages now are very different than what I went through. My former husband used to support me in my job, my studies, and in everything I did, but at home he never helped; he never changed diapers, for instance, but professionally he supported me. We do talk about women's rights at my son's and daughter's houses. I am interested that women today teach their daughters that they should fight for their rights in the future. In general, I think that women's rights in Mexico have improved. Now women can work and have more freedom than before.

Interview 14: Laura, 32 years old, graphic designer

I think feminism is the moment when women can be as they are, but there are many ideas in society that want to stop what a woman can do.

I don't know if I am a feminist. I think that's a very good question because for the moment I think of all the women who are feminists, and I don't like to be so, I don't know, how can I say . . . so dramatic with that. I do not like to have many problems with people, but there are some situations that I can't tolerate.

I think it's sad in this moment in life when there are a lot of advantages in science, in human rights, so it's impossible that there are men who cannot respect women for the way they are. Just for being human, that's the most important thing – and they need to respect that.

Yes, I know something about the feminist movement of the '70s and '80s, but I don't have a lot of the information about what happened in those years. I know many women who are the most important images in Mexico, and that they are always fighting to show to the world how important women are. So, in Mexico we have with us the image of Rigoberta Menchú. She's not a Mexican, but in all the schools, they talk about her and there are a lot of women – for example here in Mexico. In Oaxaca, Eufrosina Cruz is an image for the indigenous women who are always fighting for their rights. All the time. Every year. And it's a constant fight to be recognized by all of society that women have rights.

I think we need to fight always, all the time. It's a long fight because I think maybe 50 years ago women won the right to vote and participate in elections in Mexico for the first time. It's a shame because how old is the country and just 50 years ago women started to participate in the political life of the country? That's a shame. So, I think the movement of feminists here in Mexico of course gives us more tools to do something, and also proposes more laws about respect for women here in the country.

I think – I don't know if it's good or if it's wrong, but it's a start for something, no? Women need to fight to have their voice heard all over Mexico. It's so slow, the process, that we are starting now, and now women are more secure in doing something, with more courage to do things, and to be heard by society and to form a social movement or something to gain the attention of the government.

I think that it's a shame too, because men always have more, during those years, and now in Mexico, men have all the power too. They never relinquish power; they try to input their ideas and power into others. They don't care who suffers or who needs to die. It doesn't matter; it's just about the power. They don't want to give that up. And if there is a woman that can fight against that, of course they do everything to push her away.

In the more important cities, here in Mexico, there are movements for girls so they can choose their majors but it is not happening in all of the country. That's a reality because here in Mexico, in Mexico City, Guadalajara, and Monterrey, maybe there is more freedom, but in other States there is not that opportunity. And there is more openness to be an engineer or a scientist here in the cities but in the States, no. Including the family, it's a part of stopping women's dreams. The family, the boyfriend, the friends, or something like that. If they start to say, "Why do you do that?" or "Why do you want that?" – they start to question her, so it's a shame, and she throws away her dreams. Yes, they don't have an open mind to say "My girl can be a doctor or do something for the society." That's not happening. "She will be a wife with her children, and she will take care of her house." That's the traditional family model in Mexico.

In the cities yes, there are more chances for sexual freedom, but if they have a grandmother or grandfather, they start to get advice like, "No, he is not for you. He is not really a good man for you, he can't make you happy" and a lot of those things. All the BS. But in other States starting at 10–12 years old, they start pressuring a girl or woman to get married and that's sad, because they can't be happy children, because when they are 15 years old, they need to marry or be a mom. Can you imagine that?

There are many jobs that don't respect women, and there are many situations where if a woman is pregnant, they say goodbye to her, and they don't pay her. And they leave the office and that's it; there is no severance pay (severance pay is required by Mexican Federal Labor Law in nearly all terminations of employment). So, there are a lot of irregularities in that.

Sor Juana Inés de la Cruz is one icon for literature here in Mexico. All her writings are about differences between men and women. There is a text that says *"Hombres necios que acusáis a la mujer sin razón"* ("foolish men who accuse women without reason") – it is a popular phrase from her and of course in many books she wrote about how men are, and how they limit women. And you can imagine how that happened three centuries ago. But we are now in 2018, and it's the same situation. There have been three centuries and not a lot of progress.

Unfortunately, I think that many follow the models of the grandmothers or the mothers who don't grant freedom or confidence to their girls about doing something great or bigger, no? Because they think she can have a house, a husband, and that's all. And there is more – at a certain age, if she is not married, of course it's a problem. "Why don't you get married? Are you weird? Are you a lesbian?"

Men don't like for women to read, because then a woman can start to imagine how to make things better, no? And the other way around, when we read books for women, of course it's inspirational. You can make something better of your life. You start to dream, you start to think, "Why don't I do this?" You start to think how you can do the things you have in your mind. Where do you want to go? What do you deserve? For women, I think it's very good to make something for us, but for men – of course it's a problem.

I think I'm very fortunate because my parents always pushed me to make something of myself. So, all my education started with "You are alone. You need to learn to do whatever you want in your life. You can't wait for a man to come help you or something like that." So, if I decided something, I tried to do it until the point where I couldn't, so I needed to do something better, and of course my parents are not feminists. They think we are one society, and that we can work together. I can see men as friends I can trust, and we can work together, no? I think that's the most important thing they taught me.

Regarding learning about my own sexuality – my mother, yes, she told me. I think all the mothers in the cities talk to their daughters, like I told you, I think yes. In general, yes, she tried to open my eyes to how the world works and tried to be so smart with all the things happening around sexual topics. I think it was very good for me because I started in a school for just girls. So, when I went out and saw men and how the world worked in another way, of course it was impactful for me. And I tried to get comfortable with myself. And of course, it was really important for me.

Yes, of course Mexico is a patriarchal society. Men always want to have control, including women's partners. There is not a lot of freedom to do something. They always have to question, "Who is he? He's your friend? Maybe he wants something more with you" and you can't have the freedom to get acquainted with another person with more freedom because a man always starts thinking there is something more. And of course, if they see you doing something more successfully than them, there will be a lot of problems.

My father always talked to me about how I couldn't allow anybody to hurt me. No matter how much I love that person, they can't stop my feelings, or can't make me feel bad. I can't allow that. I need to be happy first, and of course my father says, "You need to read this book, you need to know about these laws that can protect women just in case."

I think we have the responsibility to do something for the new generations. To write books or create movements. Now with Facebook Live, something like social media, to share with all society, all the girls. To tell women that "Nobody in this world can make you feel bad. Nobody can take advantage of you." So, with all the things we have now, we can make something better for the new generations, of course. We can create courses, books, or guides, or whatever, for the girls to be always informed about rights for women.

Interview 15: Karla, 26 years old, business owner

I think feminism is a cultural mindset in which both women and men recognize that women have as much value as men. I think feminism is usually confused with women trying to retaliate against machismo, against male oppression. But I think, from my own point of view, feminism is the recognition that we are both different but valuable, and we have the same rights, same everything. I think feminism is giving women their place as valuable members of society.

Yes, exactly, I think it's about equality. It's about recognizing our differences because I also think it's crazy to think that we are the same. We are not the same, we are physically different, we are mentally different – I think it's about recognizing and celebrating our differences and making the best of them.

Yes, I consider myself a feminist. I'm an engineer. I studied to be an engineer. And with that kind of major, I think people are used to seeing engineers as men. I faced a lot of discrimination; a lot of my female peers faced a lot of discrimination because there's this social construct that tells people that engineers are maybe more reliable if they're men, and that women are not as smart or as capable of learning math, physics, any kind of science. So as a woman engineer, I have had to become a feminist because I need to stand up for myself, for my capabilities, for my intelligence, for everything I am. And I think that defending those reasons was feminism. I think if other people will not give us our place in society we need to take it for ourselves. That's what I think.

I don't know any women who fought directly for women's rights, but I know several women who fought with their actions. For example, there was one teacher I had in school who was around 60 or 70 years old – she was not an engineer, but she studied science. She was one of the first women in Mexico to study that major. She studied something about food quality. And this woman, Dr. Rojas, was a huge inspiration to me because when she studied there was no such thing as a woman in her major. She paved the way for other women to do what she did. They didn't go out with pickets and they didn't shout at men, like the traditional concept of fighting. But through actions, which I think are a lot more valuable, they did fight for feminism, and they paved the way for us to get where we are right now.

Yes, feminism has helped women obtain more rights. I think it has helped, because through feminism, I can read today, lots of women can read today, but I don't think we have the same rights. We've come a long way, but there is still a longer way to go because society has to change, the whole society. There are a lot of women who I do not consider feminists, their mindsets are kind of oppressive and they don't even realize it. I think women being able to vote is a big thing, but it's not all of it. There is a lot of domestic violence still, towards women, and the other way around, but that's not the point here. I think particularly in Mexico, feminism is clearly needed because traditionally our culture has been machista since it was founded – ever since the Spanish came and conquered and whatnot. Male oppression has been there since the beginning, and feminism has little by little – very little by little – paved the way towards a better, a more balanced gender situation in which jobs are equally available for everyone, in which a job is not associated necessarily to a gender, which is a great problem that I have personally experienced. I think men are a lot more aware of sexual harassment behaviors than they have been in the past, and they didn't even realize it was sexual harassment. I think any social change, true change, takes time, and takes perseverance and a lot of determination.

As I said before, I think everything we have achieved has been through perseverance, and I don't think men would have given us our place in society if we hadn't taken it for ourselves. I think our behaviors, our values, our convictions are what have taken us to where we are right now. Without feminism, without that conviction that we should be treated equally, that we should have the same rights, we would be right where we started.

There is an abysmal difference between poor people in Mexico, who are mostly machista, and more educated people. They have different points of view and mindsets. In general, the biggest social difference between men and women is the fact that men don't have children physically. They don't bear children, they don't breastfeed them, so that actual biological difference makes for a huge social impairment for women. Men don't need to take paternity leave in Mexico, that's not a thing, I know in other first-world countries they do. I think in Finland they do that. In Mexico people get fired because they're pregnant, I think the biggest difference is that one. I think all which relates to children is what sets women behind in Mexico, and I'm referring to a job, I mean the fathers of the kids expect the women to clean the kids, feed the kids, educate the kids, everything.

Traditionally in Mexico, men are the ones who work in the family. They have to provide everything – and I'm talking about a nice family, I'm talking about a successful family, because there are a lot of cases in Mexico in which men just bail and leave a pregnant woman or a woman with children on her own. The rate is surprisingly high for men who leave women behind with kids or when they're pregnant. It's a combination of both things; the family orientation and the fact that since the beginning, the roles have been established such as that women can't work, can't do anything but clean or cook because we are not smart enough to do certain things, or because we are not capable enough, or not strong enough.

Nowadays more and more women have access to other majors at school. Actually, I think my class at Tec de Monterrey in biotech engineering was the first one that had 52% or 54% girls – that had never happened before. It had always been male dominated. And my generation was the first one to have more girls, but still, it's a major which is socially seen as better fit for a boy. If I were talking about mechanical engineering for example, that has like a 10% girl population, no more. And still it's not very drastic, they are not bullied or anything, but people have this notion that mechanical engineering girls are not feminine or they're misfits. There's been progress I think, but as I said before: not enough.

I don't think there has been a lot of progress about sexual freedom in Mexico. I think society still condemns sexual activity outside of marriage. I think we still do it. I think maybe ideally (speaking about sexual freedom), when I think about that topic, my mom comes to my mind, or my boy-friend's mom. My mom would die, my mom would flip if she found out I had sexual activities with someone else besides my boyfriend, and his mom would too. Even though they try to be modern and open-minded, they are not, in practice. I think their values are very deep rooted. The way they were brought up is very deep rooted in their minds. I think maybe people are try-ing to make an effort, but still we're not there. I don't think there's been a lot of progress there. However, I think people have sex and say, "What the hell, I'll deal with the consequences." There is not that much fear maybe. But I think the social backlash is virtually the same.

No, I don't think men and women make the same money for the same job. Not that long ago I was watching a documentary on Netflix about wages worldwide and no, there's not a single country in the world that pays men and women equally for the same job. And maybe the wage is the same, the exact amount, the number is the same. But in reality, women maybe are asked to stay a little late to finish some job, or maybe they're asked to do something else that doesn't correspond to their work. So women end up doing more work for the same pay, which translates to less pay. I'm not an expert, that's just my viewpoint from where I am, but that's what I've heard, that's my experience, that's my street knowledge.

I know that my grandmother used to prepare a meal that resembled a menu. She had to have several dishes so that her husband and her sons could pick what they wanted to eat that day, and she had to have the house clean, and everything ready, oriented towards comforting and pampering, I would say, her husband and her sons. I think that women traditionally are expected to cook, to clean, to stay back and not give their opinions, to be reserved, we shouldn't say bad words, we shouldn't curse. There are curses which are thrice frowned upon if a woman says them. In my experiences and those of certain people that I relate to, it's okay to say certain words, but not others. For example, I wouldn't dare say them in front of my father. 2018, I'm 26 years old, and I wouldn't say those bad words in front of my father, because I know it would disappoint him. If I'm being rational, there's no difference in which words you use, it is up to you, but I myself suffer from that.

I kind of steer clear of political issues because I get too involved, and I get depressed to think how differently men treat women. It's 2018, and we still can't get treated equally, so I try to steer clear of it. I have learned about feminism, both Mexican and international. I've been part of movements, I wasn't out in the streets shouting as I said before, but I voice my concerns quite loudly on social media about insecurity and how girls can't go out by themselves at night. Maybe I don't know famous feminist writers, but regular people writing their thoughts and feelings on social media. I would bet over 90% of women in Mexico have at one point or another been sexually harassed. Either on the street or in the classroom. At Tec de Monterrey it happened to me by a teacher. A male teacher. It happened to me and it was a teacher and it was a private school, the best school in Mexico and it happened to me and it happened to a lot of other girls. I wasn't traumatized, but I wasn't happy about it either. So yeah, along with other girls, mostly on social media, I've voiced my concerns about it. Even though it disturbs me, I like reading about it, I like exchanging thoughts with other women about it because it makes me feel like I'm not alone about this. Maybe it's not a very established trending topic like "Me Too" but it is more and more every day. You get posts on social media. For example, I shared this on social media repeatedly: if you are getting kidnapped or sexually harassed, go near another woman. Take her hand. If you are in trouble, know that you can take my hand, and I will take care of you and we will go through it together, I will help you get out of the situation. None of us should be alone; we should band together.

Ever since I was a little girl my parents always told me I could be anything. They enrolled me in different extracurricular activities – for example, I remember I took ballet and basketball at the same time which were thought of as girl and boy activities. I had the great fortune of being raised not religiously and not with gender roles, so that I could always be what I wanted to be. My father for example, he studied engineering too, and he was a commercial pilot. He fixes everything, and he taught me how to weld, how to do woodcraft, like a solid door, I can do that. He taught me about cars. For example, car issues, in Mexico, if you see a woman with her head inside the hood of a car, the reaction of a lot of people is to kick the woman out because she will screw something up. My dad taught me that I wasn't stupid or impaired. I could do whatever the hell I wanted to do, and they taught me a lot of things. As many things as they could, associated with both genders, so one day I could pick anything I wanted to be, anything I wanted to do. I'm super grateful to my parents for that. They never ever said "No you can't do that because you're a girl." Not a single time. "You can't wear that because you're a girl." Not ever. . . . I had my Barbies and I had He-Man, or an action figure. So, I had both girl and boy toys. I had science sets for kids, I grew up thinking that being a girl was not a disadvantage at all. I think it helped me be who I am today and to have the confidence to stand up to other people and say, "I'm not disabled because I'm a girl," I'm different and have different capacities but not less valuable, only different. That's what they taught me.

Actually, I think my mother did a very poor job talking to me about sexuality because she made me feel super uncomfortable. Looking back, I feel that there were better ways to talk about it. She talked about sexuality maybe a little too much. She inflicted this fear on me that I shouldn't walk in my underwear inside of the house because people outside of the house would look at me and come rape me. That's what she said to me, so I always lived with this fear of walking around in my underwear, let alone naked. She kind of rushed through the subject, not very in depth because I think she was uncomfortable too. I mean it's normal. Parents are heartbroken to see that their kids are no longer kids – that their kids are having sex. Fathers root for their boys to have sex all the time but not for girls. Although it was uncomfortable, I did have the correct guidance, and what I didn't know I found out quite easily. I think that every woman should talk about her sexuality to her children – both boys and girls. I also think it's important to state to boys that women are not their playthings, it's important for boys to know how to ask for consent and how to interpret it, so when it's no, it's no and vice versa. A lot of women in Mexico – poor people in Mexico don't even know how pregnancy works. They just wake up and their bellies are full. They don't even know how it happened. I think it's terrible that people don't even know how they get pregnant, let alone other stuff. The very fact that people don't even know how we procreate, it's alarming. I think everyone, both adult and kids, should get sexual information. I think we should stop making it into a terrible scary thing, and removing the sin factor, because religion is a big part of it, in Mexico at least. Religion is a huge part of how people live their daily lives. Absolutely, my boyfriend's mom is super religious, super.

I think Mexico, particularly Mexico City is moderately patriarchal because I think we still have a lot of things. Like, we have come a long way, as I said before, I think we have come a long way. I think, for example, more and more men are starting to step up for women when other men are harassing them. I've seen my own boyfriend defending other girls from boys who are harassing them. Little by little I've seen examples of progress towards equality, but I think we still have a long way to go. I think Mexican machismo is known worldwide. Men call women whores or sluts – *putas* – without regard, like they're calling them a girl, like it's a synonym. *Perra* (bitch), they like that word. I hate it. *Puta madre*, all the time. I try to consider myself a feminist. I try not to do it, but it's a reflex, I go "*puta madre*." We have been advancing toward equality in some regards and not so much in others.

We don't talk directly about women's rights, not like an after-dinner topic. Actually, my employee thinks my mom and I are weak, that he should carry everything for us. But for example, my mom, when somebody discriminates against her gender, she'll flip, get angry, and tell everyone off, and show that she can do it, that she is capable. Not directly, but through actions, through a mindset. I know I've said that word like a thousand times now but that's what it is. A state of consciousness in which you don't view women as weak or unable. Yeah, not directly but through actions, through everyday . . . it's been a huge fight of mine explaining to people that I'm an engineer. They don't even realize I can do math, that I know physics and stuff. I know about physics, and every time I say something that reveals what I know, my employees or maybe the people visiting here can't even believe it. It's very difficult for them to process the fact that I have knowledge about it.

I think through our actions is how we pave the way for other women, through example. I myself am an engineer, and I graduated with a lot of other girls who also are engineers. I know I repeat that a lot, but that's my case, I paved the way for other girls to say, "They did it, why shouldn't I?" I think the fact that we are doing what we're doing, fighting for our rights, is leaving a precedent for future women to realize they shouldn't do stuff the way men have traditionally done them. I think we are doing something, leaving a legacy.

Interview 16: Ariana, 26 years old, consultant for a software company

Well, yes. I consider myself to be a feminist because personally I broke out of what is imposed on us by society in Mexico. I searched for other roles. Not a housewife role, I looked to better myself, to study and take on other roles that any man can perform. I grew up in a town where things change going from a town to a city. In a town, it is very difficult for a woman to keep studying. Most of the women get married, have kids, and take on the housewife role and don't look for anything else. I left the town and came to the city a couple of years ago, and I started looking for another role, I didn't want to be a housewife in a house with kids and a husband. I was interested in looking farther ahead into a professional role, to start studying and gaining professional knowledge.

Directly, I don't know about the feminist movement in Mexico in the 1970s or 80s. I have heard of the movement or similar things, but I've never been in direct contact with it. As far as female friends around me, I try to offer my support according to what I have been through. I give them advice, I have always offered to help. For example, I have a friend from my town who got married and things were not going well with her husband. I offered her the opportunity to come live with me, so she could keep studying. I gave her that opportunity, but many women fear change, I don't know. I'm very adventurous, and many women are still scared. She didn't want the change, so she is still with her husband. For example, she didn't want to keep studying or doing other things, and I don't think she is happy. I offered to help with what I could, but she did not accept it.

Today, I see things are more equal for women, thanks to feminism. Sometimes we have a lot of obstacles placed on us in companies because they think that we can't perform the same way as men, I have actually run into a type of boss that did not like to hire women because he said women brought in too many problems, that we fought a lot, we have to go to children's activities, or the kids get sick, or personal things. So he wanted to hire only men. But in my experience, I see that it is getting easier now in jobs. We can obtain better positions, like a man, but it has taken a lot of work. In my case, I am an equal to other men, so I think that yes, it has improved a lot. In my town I have still not seen a change like that. Normally, life is still the same there; the housewife and the man working outside of the house. There are women doing certain roles outside of the house, but it is not seen as much as it is in the city.

No, I don't think women would have gained more rights in Mexican society without the feminist movement and without the efforts of other Mexican women that fought for more rights. I believe that to achieve any change there needs to be initiative and action. Fortunately, it's so good that there have been these movements, and that we women have proved that we can also have other roles.

Well, to a certain extent, when it comes to work, men still have more rights. I think that men still get more preference for important positions, like executives. However, women do also have the opportunities to get to those positions, even though we have more obstacles.

At this time, women have more freedom to enter into higher education than before. I have seen that women can enter fields that only men were in before, in this case, engineering. Before, it was a man's area and now we see more women. I have a female acquaintance who is an engineer. She has her company and has many women working for her that are engineers. And as women we can get to those positions that were reserved for men.

Fortunately, here in the city they no longer prohibit you from entering certain fields because you are a woman. We have that freedom to decide.

I don't believe that women have more sexual freedom outside of marriage in Mexico today. I believe that society still condemns sexual activity outside of marriage for women. If we go to the provinces, the truth is that everything is very closed and rigid. You are judged very much in that sense, you are judged for sexual freedom outside of marriage. You are judged as well if you are a single mother. My grandparents and my parents are especially like that about sex outside of marriage. You are judged a lot. In the city it changes a bit more, there is not so much judging, even though there are certain criticisms but not in the same degree as in the provinces.

No, I don't believe that in Mexico women receive the same salary as men for the same amount of work. Men get more money; however, there are companies that do pay the same salary. In my case, I have gotten the same salary as other male coworkers, but it is rare. As I mentioned before, as a woman you have more obstacles, but you do have the opportunity to earn a high salary.

Well, traditionally in Mexico there is always the housewife role, where you cook, you tend to the children, tend to the husband, and now it has changed because they both work, but unfortunately the woman usually still has to cover her role in the house as well as in her professional role. There is still not 100% equality. As a woman you need to always have a clean house, prepare the kids for school, have the house organized, and do well at work. But the woman still has a heavier load; the mother role and the working role.

No, I don't know Mexican female writers that identify as feminists. The truth is that I am not very involved in the topic of feminism and who has fought. I grew up in a very small town called Tuxtla, in Michoacán, where everyone knows each other, and where society is still very judgmental. There is more machismo, and the culture is about the housewife and the husband who works outside of the home. Since it is such a small town everyone sees how you live and what you do. It is very judgmental. You are judged if you are single, or if you are 18 or 19, they ask when you will get married and why you haven't gotten married. So from a young age they want to plant the idea to look for a husband. There are a lot of young girls who are 16 or 17 and have children already.

Well, in my case my education at home was traditional because I was a girl. I'm not sure about my parents, but someone who had a big influence in my life was my aunt. Like I said before, my dad is very misogynistic, and when I wanted to leave the house, they did not want to support me since I wanted to go study in the city. They did not give me support, and would tell me that I had to adapt to what they gave me, and my dad is still that way. My influence was an aunt who told me to keep studying and changed that custom. My mom is a bit more open too, so she did not prohibit me from leaving the home, but I still did not receive economic support. They said I left and decided not to adapt to what they could give me so that was it. Here in the city it was my aunt that gave me a place to stay, and she is the one who had other ideas because she was already working and saw professionals and she had another vision which she transmitted to me.

No, my mom never talked to me about sexuality, which has always made me sad. She never mentioned anything. I learned as time passed and my aunts were the ones who spoke with me about it. I have an aunt who is five years older than me, and she told me everything, and I also learned from friends, but not my mom. I think it is important as a mother or a father to communicate with your children, so if you learn things in the house, none of the things you hear will surprise you and you will be prepared for comments from other people. At the end of the day, what happened was that since my mom never spoke about it with me, everything was new for me, and I learned it from other sources, and it was not nice at all.

For the most part, yes, Mexican society is patriarchal, the man dominates. There are cases where men are more submissive, but mostly, yes, the man dominates. Right now, I don't have a partner. At my parents' house, women's rights are never discussed. The man dominates there, my dad is very misogynistic. My mom has a more open mind. She is more about not being dumb, and about a woman not depending on a man. Since she has lived through it all these years with my dad, she doesn't want us to end up like that. My sister and me.

Yes, of course I would like for Mexican women to leave a legacy to their daughters, for them to stop having that dependence on a man. What I have seen is that marriages aren't working anymore. Before, marriages lasted for years. My grandparents are still together and so are my parents. And now marriages fail. Because men's culture does not allow them to accept that a woman can perform equally to them or that she can earn more than him. I don't know how to explain, but I would like machismo to end. I am very happy with my professional life, so I couldn't be a housewife. We should leave behind a culture in which women can't develop professionally. I think it would be beneficial to the whole society since we can be as productive as men in our professional lives. We can also contribute to the economic development of our country, not just men.

Now I have been given the same opportunities as men according to the skills I have acquired. I have had the same opportunities. The position I am in can be done by a man or a woman. The salary is the same for both. Also, I have had experiences with the law, and here in Mexico there is a lot of corruption. Once, I was arguing with an ex-boyfriend. A policeman came over because he was assaulting me, and the policeman told me that I was the crazy one, and that I was drunk when I had not even had a drink. He gave my boyfriend preference and it was a bad experience.

Interview 17: Alicia, 64 years old, housewife

I think that feminism is a movement that has always existed, century after century, but it has never been allowed to have so much strength as it does now. Women have fought a lot more for their rights, so this has been growing as time has gone on. I feel that women are becoming more and more independent, and they can achieve their goals without the support of a man. If they want to reach for the moon, they can do it themselves. Frida Kahlo said that once and it has stayed with me because I think that we as women have a huge capacity to achieve what we want without the need for someone to do it for us. I feel that that's what a feminist movement is, and to be next to a man, with the same equality in everything: family, home, work, children, to be united in a spiritual way it's even better; and if not, to respect the spirituality of each one.

   I consider myself a woman born in a different time, not a feminist. Because at my age, many women have achieved what I would have wanted to achieve. I would have wanted to have a university education, to have developed myself in other ways, maybe I would have – I don't know. I feel that I had the capacity to do other things, but I was in such an enclosed circle, that I focused only on what I had been taught – that I had to be a good mother, a good daughter, a good wife, and to care for my family. And I was too old when I realized that it didn't have to be that way. I had many emotional problems because you face something that you had never wanted to face or that you had never even seen. When you realize that it exists you say, "Well, what am I doing in this world?" I think I don't consider myself a feminist person, but I would have liked to have done something when I was younger, along with a man who had the capacity to recognize a woman with the liberty to do what she wanted to do. I would have liked that. But circumstances were different, and it was not this way. That's why I think I am a person ahead of these times, because many women at my age think and do different things. And I feel that I think and do different things than they do.

   Yes, I have heard about feminist movements; especially in the United States when women fought for their right to vote, because before, women did not have the right. I used to hear that women were fighting for their right to vote. Maybe I did not have enough of the ability to understand what they were really looking for, but I would hear that it was a feminist movement searching for the right to vote, that their voices became a reality and influenced the decisions of the government. Well, that's what I would hear, and afterwards I focused on other things, but I was never involved. Maybe through books, for example Ángeles Mastretta, who I consider a woman with whom I have sometimes felt like I can relate to about many things. But she had the great blessing, or however you want to call it, to have been born into a family that was well adjusted, with wealth, so she could then develop herself. But in some other things I feel that I would have enjoyed living her life, because I like it. Another one is Frida Kahlo. Curiously, Frida Kahlo died the year in which I was born. I learned about her story and saw that she was such a fierce woman, and such a free woman in every aspect. She lived how she wanted to, and she did not care how she was, or the consequences that she would suffer – and she was a woman that suffered a lot, physically. But a woman that "flew even though she had no feet." Even though she could not walk, because that was her spirit, to fly. So that made me relate to her a lot. Maybe that's why I feel that I feel out of my time.

Well, I worked for a short period of time, so I don't know about discrimination in the workplace. The place where I worked was very nice. For me it was a place that gave me the opportunity to grow, it was a place that gave me the opportunity to study an X, Y, or Z career like translation, but it was a place that allowed me to do things like travel, get to know other worlds and gain economic independence. For me it was a very satisfying workplace. It gave me a lot. I did not see any type of abuse. I never saw it there. Maybe because it was a UN institution, where there was a lot of European influence, so that surely had something to do with it. It wasn't completely Mexican, so the "macho" Mexican – no. The people who were there were very well educated and there was a lot of influence from the UN. So maybe that's why I had a good job from that perspective. I never saw any abuse or anything out of the ordinary there.

Unfortunately, even we Mexicans discriminate a lot against our own people. Sometimes skin color is a motive to discriminate against someone. Instead of looking at the value of the person they look at the physical aspects, and I have seen it a lot. I have lived it, not personally – but I have seen other people treated badly due to their physical appearance, their economic situation, their skin color, their culture, their ideology, their beliefs, and they are then minimized because we think that since we were born in a city or work in a company, or because we have certain privileges, we are superior to others and I don't agree with that.

Well, I was a mother to two daughters. I didn't have any boys, so maybe unconsciously instead of thinking of how to teach them to use a broom, how to clean, and how to make fried beans, I wanted them to worry about studying, about moving ahead, and about having a career. I didn't care if they knew how to wash or iron, they'll see the consequences when they have to do it in their own homes because they will surely do it. But as a mother I did not give them that training, if you can call it that. So, at home there were no misogynistic or feministic rules, or matriarchy or patriarchy. I think that in my personal case there was more decision making, I had to make more decisions, but nothing else. There was no abuse of anything.

Growing up at home was different. We were four women and four men. The oldest was a half-brother but we never saw him as a half-brother, there was always the idea that he was just another sibling and we were eight all together. I feel that there was a lot of influence on my mother's side, that the women had to tend to the men. There was the tendency for us women to serve them, do the chores, prepare things, and why? Because it was expected that further into the future we would marry, and that was the dynamic that we would face. The men were educated to receive what was given to them and some of them excelled, and some of them thought that that wasn't supposed to be the life of a woman, and it makes me happy despite what we experienced as a family – which I think was a very close-knit family. I think that we started to value each other not when we were young, but as we got older and to know that the only thing that could keep us united was love. We lost our mother at a very young age, but my father did a good job of always keeping us close. We could count on each other.

Yes, there were differences between boys and girls as kids. For us girls they did not make us do hard things or carry heavy loads or load brooms into a truck, no. But we had the responsibility of the house, the chores, the cleaning, to help my mom do things around the house. What is true is that my father was always very loving towards all of us. Very loving, and he always had the right advice for each one of us, even though we lived through things at different times.

Yes, I remember talking to my mom about my sexuality growing up. I don't know how it was with my sisters, I really don't. They married young, and I married when I was a bit older, but my relationship with my mom was very open. That's why I say that I feel like I was a bit different. Because I innocently would tell my mom, even though I was 17, "Oh mom, every time that my boyfriend kisses me my underwear gets wet." With that frankness and with that naturalness of someone who doesn't know why those things happen. I wish I would have had someone who told me before, "You know what? When you have a boyfriend you can have this, this, and that occur to you. Why? Because your hormones are racing." And it's natural for all those things to happen, but I think that I had this big openness with my mom due to my personality, and due to everything that I have told you that I have felt deep down. So, I would go to my mom and talk to her about sexual things and she would say "Oh, Licha!" because it embarrassed her more than me. And we would joke, and she would say, "Be quiet" because she would feel more embarrassed than me. And I saw it naturally. I don't know how it was with my sisters. I don't know if my mom was already open, or if it was each of us that had that openness because of personality or the chats we had with her.

When it came to my own family, I tried to be as open as possible. If they asked me directly what they wanted to know, I would tell them. If not, I wasn't going to answer questions that they had not asked. Why feed someone if they don't have teeth to chew? So, if they asked me something directly, I would see what I could do to make them understand without alarming them. Additionally, with their dad we always kissed and hugged in front of them. So, for them it was always something natural. But many times, for example with the oldest daughter, I told her "Your underwear will get wet when Roberto is kissing you."

It makes me very happy that it is now possible to talk about all of this. I like it even more now that my daughters are adults and I can tell them many things because they have their own criterion, and common sense. They are adult women and maybe they don't know everything I do, because I have lived more than half of their lives, but it gives me the impression that they have very coherent ideas about their lives, and I like that because I think that they will be good women and have good children. Not good in a religious sense, no. As human beings that know how to love others because of their value, the values people have, which is what matters the most. I think my daughters have that. About feminist movements, I am completely in agreement. It's great that women fight against oppression. It isn't possible that at this point, there are still women who must cover their faces in other countries, or women who are stoned to death because they dared to look somewhere else. It's unbelievable, to me it is a crime, but I will leave this world, and I hope that women keep fighting and that they achieve, truly achieve, their rights on the level that they deserve.

I can think of Frida Kahlo as a feminist woman. Well, there are more, but I would have to think for a while about it. What I would like for the future is that they (women) go together hand in hand. If they demand a right, to know that there is also an obligation when asking for that right. To do what they want, without asking if it is right or correct, or incorrect. Simply that they develop as human beings, so they can be happy because nobody is perfect, and nobody comes to look for perfection. We search for happiness, and we get happiness through what we do. If you get happy washing a plate all day, then wash a plate all day because you will be happy. If whatever you want to do makes you happy, then do it, because nothing will give you happiness except for yourself. Nobody will give it to you, nobody will place it in your hands. If you don't look for it, you don't find it.

Interview 18: Marta Angelica, 42 years old, software engineer manager

Well, from my own perspective feminism is kind of a movement to try to have equal rights and opportunities as a male. I think I would consider myself a feminist, and that is because I think that women and men have the same rights and should have the same opportunities, and that we should look for equality; it's like I try to push back on the misogyny. That's what it means for me. Feminist, I think I am, yeah.

No, I really don't know anything about the feminist movement in Mexico from the 1970s and 1980s. I don't remember women that have fought to better social conditions for other women in the country. I'm not well versed on that fight in Mexico.

My perspective is that feminism has helped Mexican women currently achieve the same rights as men. However, no, I don't think we have the same rights today. I think we do have them in theory, but not in practice. And I think that we hear very different stories between the big cities like Guadalajara, Mexico City, Monterrey, and the rest of the country.

I think that everything that has happened has to do a lot with what most women have fought for and with every achievement for women in Mexico, it opens the way for the rest of us. Women have achieved more rights in Mexican society, with the feminist movement and fighting for such rights.

In terms of the rights and responsibilities that are shared equally amongst men and women in Mexico, I think we have in theory, we have the right to go to school, to work, to be treated equally as well. I think those are the rights we have. I don't think that everyone in our society respects all these rights and because that's mostly in theory, otherwise we wouldn't have such high levels of crime against women.

Yes. It is my opinion that men still have more rights in Mexico. We, both (male and female) have the right to go to school for instance; however, there are still a lot of parents unable to understand that women need to go to school, that still happens. There is also the right to have a safe environment, and that is something that is not happening for women.

I think there is more freedom regarding school and university for women than there was before, yes, and I also think most of the universities are promoting that, which is a good thing. However, there are not enough women who choose to attend university. I think that universities in general work hard in making a good effort to attract more women, to retain women and have them in college. I think that is happening; however, I think we should start with those efforts earlier in life, for elementary and middle school girls. I think yes, definitely. there is more access for women in Mexico today to study fields like engineering, certain sciences, maybe even business and other subjects, majors that are traditionally for men.

I think that today in Mexico, women have more sexual freedom as far as their sexual actions and activities outside of marriage than before, maybe it's more open than it used to be. I don't know how much, I cannot measure how much it has changed from the past, but I think that society is more open, or women now are more open and trying to have the right to have more freedom in that area.

I really don't know if women receive the same salary as men for the same job in Mexico. I would say that there are areas that don't receive the same salary. But since I have spent most of my life in an international corporation, I think these corporations have been trying to reduce that salary inequality, but I don't know for a fact. I always hear that there is a difference for the same job, but in my experience, I don't have that, and my opinion would be only an opinion. I don't have the facts for that. We try to have it more equal in an international company.

Yes, in Mexico there is still a strong feeling and influence from society about the traditional roles of women. I think we still have the same idea that it doesn't matter if the woman or wife works, it is still seen as "You have to take care of the kids, you have to do the laundry, you have to do all the housework," and I think it is something very deep in the minds of society. There is something that I think is at the point where each of the couples are finding more balance and a way to change that, but I think that it's because all the guys that are married now, they were raised with that state of mind.

Again, this is my opinion; I think that women should work. The people I know, most of them have chosen to work because they want to have a better life. We have that option and we take it. I can tell you about one person with a university degree. She started to work, saw that she could have more opportunities, saw she could improve the level of life for her kids and she decided not to stop working. For my case, and I think for most of my female coworkers, we could have the choice of not working, but we prefer a better life than having the life only one income can provide. I think that for most women that I know, it is a choice of a better life, not something that you *have* to do. You can choose to live with one income, but we choose to do it the other way. We are choosing to have a better life, that's why we work instead of the other way.

I don't know any of the Mexican female writers that identify themselves as feminists. I have read some journalists, but they have written about "las muertas de Juárez" (the dead women of Juárez) or the cases of women that are prostitutes, but I don't think they are feminists. They are journalists that are focusing on issues that affect a lot of women in Mexico. But feminists that they define to be feminists, no. I don't have any author I have read about.

I don't know if education in my house as a little girl was more traditional in regard to me being a woman and taking on traditional gender roles of the Mexican woman. My case was a conflicting one because in theory we were motivated to do things. Ever since I can remember, I recall that I wanted to attend university. That was an idea that was planted in my brain; I don't know when, but as far back as I can recall, I remember that. My father didn't tell us we could not do something, but the actions were totally the opposite. My brother was the one my father took to Mexican wrestling, he was the one he took to other places, he went out with his male friends, and he would never invite us as women. Also, it was not only my father, my mother too. They allowed the boys in our house to swear, but girls couldn't say those words. We were never told explicitly that we could not do things that men could do, but their actions were very different. However, since the theory I received from my grandfather that I could do whatever I wanted to do, I never thought I couldn't do anything a man could, but it was a conflict I had when I was a kid. In theory I saw I could do things, but in practice I was not allowed to do most of the things that men could.

First, yes. My mother used to talk with me a little about my sexuality. She tried to do that. I don't think she had the correct words because for instance, one of the conversations was to not have intercourse until marriage and stuff like that. But, she did that to help. I have a daughter myself, and I think that is a conversation you should have. Mexican mothers should talk to their daughters about sexuality.

Yes, Mexican society is profoundly patriarchal. Like I said, it's changing in this city, but the rest of our country is another story. We still focus completely on men. I think we are trying to fight against that, and I know a lot of other adults agree and have changed their minds, but I think that this is only a few segments of the population; most of the population is the other way around. My husband is a university professor, and always supports my daily professional and personal life.

We do speak about the rights of women in my family. With my husband, we have a similar way of thinking, and we talk a lot, but I think it is a daily topic with him. We talk about that almost every day. With my parents no. My father has a very different way of thinking and my mother – we do that a little but not much.

I think yes, definitely, Mexican women today should leave a legacy for their daughters about the rights of Mexican women in society! I can tell you regarding my sister, she has a daughter that is 12, and she already has a different way of thinking and that is something I also want to give my daughter, so I think yes.

I have a very good experience in relation to the achievement of women's rights in Mexico. I have access to a VP, vice president of my company, and she is a woman. I have access to a couple of directors and several managers and my coworkers. I think it is a very good example of that. Also, I have my experience with my husband. The way that he thinks is also something that, in my opinion is very different than it used to be some years ago. I think we have achieved a lot of things like going to university, getting good jobs, and helping other women maintain their jobs and balance that with their family time.

Interview 19: Sofia Sanchez, 37 years old, dance teacher and office assistant

To me feminism is a way of thinking that women have about men. And, yes in some respects I consider myself a feminist. For example, in the sense that women have always been left behind in past years, it is time to be acknowledged as an equal to men. I think women and men have the same worth, not that women are worth more than men.

I don't know anything about the feminist movement in Mexico in that time period of the '70s, and '80s. I know about more contemporary women, like in this era, maybe some ten years back. Like Rigoberta Menchú, Frida Kahlo – well, she is from before. But more recently I have heard about it through social media, Facebook. I have a notion of a more contemporary feminism.

I believe feminism has helped today's Mexican women achieve the same rights as men. For example, the right to vote, the right to decide about reproductive and sexual health. Yes, of course. These rights would not have been achieved without the feminist movement and without other women that have fought for them. Definitely not, I'm sure.

In terms of rights and responsibilities, I think men and women equally share those. I think it is now more, even more now, when it comes to salaries, economics, chores at home, children. I think it is more equal now. I know that there is a difference between the salaries men and women earn in Mexico, but I think that each day it is less. There are more opportunities to develop professionally on an equal level. Maybe, yes, the difference in Mexico and Latin America is more pronounced. In cities women receive the same salary as men for the same work. In rural communities or small towns, we still see that misogyny.

There is more openness; women have more freedom of education now than before, they have more access to careers that are focused on men. But I think that there is still a lot of discrimination from male students towards female students. Universities have opened their doors to women, but it is the male classmates that make obstacles.

About sexual freedom that is not tied to marriage I think the situation is different between cities and rural communities. In cities there is much more sexual and reproductive health education, which doesn't exist in rural communities. There, women are still condemned for sex outside of marriage.

Well, in Mexico there is still a strong societal influence about the traditional roles that women must play, that women must tend to the men, the fathers, brothers, nephews, obviously the children. They must cook, clean, care for the house and in some cases, it is double the work. They must go to work, and come back to care for the house, husband, everything. At home I was educated about freedom. My parents taught me that I could do the same things as a man.

Yes, my mother discussed my sexuality with me. I think it is correct to talk with girls about this topic. Mexican society is deeply patriarchal. It is a society that is traditionally misogynistic. Mexico has always been about the traditional Mexican "macho," and it is hard to knock down such obstacles.

I am married, and my husband supports me in my daily and professional life. I support him as well. No, in my home and my parents' home, women's rights are not discussed because it is an implicit topic. Pablo, my husband has always been about "I don't have to do different things just because I am a man." It has always been equal. We both wash dishes, we both do laundry, we both care for our daughter. It is not a topic we have to discuss, it is implicit.

What I would like for today's Mexican women to leave as a legacy to their daughters or women of the future, in relation to Mexican women and their rights, is that we speak more, and speak publicly about these rights, about equality. I think women are equally capable to do any work, any chore and also to study. To speak about and convey it [equality] as a way of living, not just a way of thinking, and that it [equality] can transcend generations.

My direct experiences in relation to women's rights here in Mexico is that I had access to a university education. My parents paid for it just like my brother's, and we both went to college. I had the freedom to marry the person I chose, and I decided when to have my first and only daughter. And I was from the time when women could still go out on the streets without anything happening to us. Now it is not so safe as a woman or teenager.

My parents didn't protect me more compared to my brother about who could go out. No. We could both go out freely, but times have changed. There are more kidnappings, there is more trafficking of women. When I was a teenager, this did not happen. My brother and I would go out together or separately without a problem or any fear.

5   Final analysis

The interviews presented here demonstrate that these women stand apart in some of their views on several topics but agree on numerous others. The differences in education, professional careers, jobs, personal upbringing, and development within Mexican society are evident in such an assortment of women from diverse social backgrounds in the country. Irrespective of education or social status, an important number of these interviewees enjoyed expanding upon certain themes and would often stray from our topic at hand. In so doing, these women demonstrated how they consider their lived personal experiences significant enough to be part of their narratives. They impregnate their lived experiences with such an array of social and personal consciousness, that if they stray off topic, it is because they need their voices to be heard. They have most assuredly been silent for many years, regardless of any feminist social movement in the country.

There is an alarming scarcity of polls or interviews with "common" Mexican women throughout the past. However, in 2004, Cecilia Olivares[1] conducted a small series of interviews with academicians and students of Women's Studies in Mexico about feminism and its impact in society. These were hardly the "common" woman. The scarcity of this type of information demonstrates how invisible the "common" Mexican woman is within the context of Mexican feminism. The interviews in this book, with this particular group of "common" Mexican women are a small sample of the impact, or absence thereof, of the Mexican feminist movement of the 1970s and 1980s on women in the country. It is a tiny illustration, but as representatives of the specific groups of women to which each interviewee belongs, we can try to make hypothetical comments about the results of the movement's influence on nonacademic women of low social standing who are not intellectuals.

Although many of these women do not consider themselves to be or realize that they are feminists, the differences in beliefs amongst these women are palpable. Such discrepancies start with Olivia, who doesn't consider herself a feminist: "I define myself to be more inclusive than feminist" she says, and Gabriela, who openly declares: "I personally think of myself as a feminist." These positions will indeed establish Mexican women's different views concerning the feminist movement and its advancements in the country.

The main concern of this study is to see how (and whether) the feminist movement of the 1970s and 1980s influenced "common" women. Only a slight percentage of those interviewed expressed "hearing" about the women's movement of those decades and of other women in the past who fought for women's rights, as well as others who still fight for women's rights in the country in all social areas. There are several who agree that some precursors of the movement did have an impact on present-day women although they don't know who they were. There are women who, because of their age, lived through the 1970s and 1980s; however, they don't have any recollection at all about the feminist movement. The younger women don't have any memories about it or have never heard about it. Lucila, who is 67 years old, very emphatically mentions: "I don't know anything about the Mexican feminist movement from the '70s and '80s. I don't remember anything." Clara, who is in her fifties, states: "I don't know anything about the feminist movement that took place during the '70s and '80s in Mexico."

It is, indeed, extremely interesting to see that only an imperceptibly small segment, or almost none, of these "common" Mexican women is aware of this feminist movement. We are led to believe, then, that in fact, since its origins, the Mexican feminist movement has belonged to women of the upper classes who neglected to share anything with other women of lower classes in the country because their demands were not the same as, for instance, those of the indigenous or working-class women. In 1996, a few years after the tumultuous times of the feminist movement of the 1970s and 1980s, Gabriela Cano[2] traced a century of life of the Mexican feminist movement from the late nineteenth century to the late twentieth century. In her article, Cano reviews all the most significant actions and literature that feminist women in the country have produced during this time. Through her work, we see that the movement's leaders were women of the educated upper classes who established newspapers, journals, organized conferences, and other activities associated with women of their status. With respect to the decade of the 1970s, Cano explains that "The force that prompted the movement was the search for freedom inspired by the counterculture in university environments . . . influenced by the movement of women's liberation from the United States" ("*El feminismo tomó vuelo nuevamente a principios de los años setenta en medio de búsquedas libertarias inspiradas por la contracultural en ambientes universitarios . . . fue decisiva la influencia del movimiento de liberación de la mujer en los Estados Unidos*") (354). The movement, Cano says, only "interested a few people, most of them women from middle and upper classes, with college education" ("*Interesaba a muy pocas personas, en su mayor parte, mujeres de estratos medios, con educación universitaria*"). Cano continues and says that in the '80s, "feminism took off in the academic world . . . which increased until the end of the century" ("*En los años ochenta despegó el feminismo en el terreno académico, proceso que va en aumento al aproximarse el fin de siglo*") (355).

Throughout the years, the demands of these Mexican women involved with the movement have focused on women's right to vote, access to all areas of society such as politics and education, women's right to work without their husbands' consent, the right to divorce, access to contraception, and others. These demands were not related to the necessities of the peasants, blue-collar workers, and women of the lower social classes, but differed greatly as we have seen in Chapter 3, dedicated to the Mexican context. It shouldn't surprise us, then, that these interviewed women have no knowledge of the feminist movement of the 1970s and 1980s.

It is evident why Mexico is often called the land of "machismo." We only have to look at disparities in salary that affect a vast majority of women doing the same job as men as well as the glass ceiling that still denies them access to high-paying positions in upper-level management. Additionally, a governmental indifference and apathy still exists toward offering legal protections and benefits to domestic help, a predominantly female profession. Even though men today are still seen as breadwinners and women as housewives and caregivers, women have won the right to attend college and study a much larger variety of majors, not only those traditionally tailored to suit women such as elementary education and nursing. Most of our interviewees concur with the fact that men earn better salaries than women in similar positions, even when women boast higher levels of education and experience. Goretti Flores, who for instance, went through this shocking experience:

> there are still many jobs where a woman earns less than a man in the same position. So, in the last two years, I have been twice unemployed and have come across that situation where men earn more than me for the same job. . . . You see, on the topic of discrimination, in that part, like I have just told you, that's the way it was at my last job. We started at the same time, one man and one woman and he made more than me. I became good friends with him, so we had all the confidence and openness to ask, "How much did they hire you for?" and we were doing the same thing in the same area, etc. He earned more than me. He earned 4,000–5,000 pesos ($210–260USD) per month more than me, so it was a very significant difference for the same job.

Marta Angelica has had a different experience, pointing out that she works for an international company in Mexico:

> I really don't know if women receive the same salary as men for the same job in Mexico. I would say that there are areas that don't receive the same salary. But since I have spent most of my life in an international corporation, I think these corporations have been trying to reduce that salary inequality, but I don't know for a fact. I always hear that there is a difference for the same job, but in my experience, I don't have that, and my opinion would be only an opinion. I don't have the facts for that. We try to have it more equal in an international company.

Goretti Flores and Marta Angelica have, at least, a bachelor's degree which brings more opportunities for them; however, a few of our other interviewees, although they are college graduates, have not been so fortunate, not to mention those whose level of education is very low, thus impeding them from accessing professional jobs. In 2018, Maria Camarena Adame and Maria Luisa Saavedra Garcia[3] published a compelling article on women in high-profile positions working for Mexican and international companies, which presents interesting findings about female executives and CEOs. The authors say that: "Even though women have increased their participation in the job market, their position is at a disadvantage compared to men's" ("*A pesar de que la mujer ha aumentado su participación en el mercado de trabajo en las ultimas décadas, su position es de desventaja con respecto a sus compañeros*") (322). An important fact that the authors state is that: "In 2012, the number of women in vulnerable jobs (family business without pay, or self-employed) was 50%" ("*Para el año 2012, la proporción de mujeres en empleo vulnerable (trabajadores familiares no remunerados y trabajadores por cuenta propia) era de 50%*") (323). What we can see is that low-educated "common" women must rely on self-reliance to provide for themselves and their families; whereas, men have more access to formal jobs. It seems like Mexico is still a country with a culture that believes that women's work is at home and, that women who work are less valuable than men. This article is very important for the new vision and data it offers in terms of employment for women in present day Mexico; nevertheless, it fails to mention that women still earn less than men even in the same positions as described by some of our interviewees.

"Common" Mexican women are not very aware of the rights achieved by the feminist movement. They mention that women in the past and present have made it possible for them to obtain equality with men in some areas of society such as politics, culture, and education. However, they can't name anyone specifically, either a writer, poet, academic professor, intellectual, or social activist who could have had some influence on them. It seems that everything related to women's rights is born in the academic world and through publications by researchers and well-established intellectuals whose works don't reach "common" women. One author, for instance, Miriam Lang[4] finds that any women who have worked within the feminist movement in Mexico have reached certain positions of power in NGOs (non-governmental organizations); the author clarifies that

> only women with a certain level of education and cultural knowledge could satisfy the demands of these funding agencies. It is therefore a fact that NGOs offer a professional point of view outside the traditional job markets and self-realization only to especially well-educated women and generally those from middle and upper classes (*Sólo mujeres con cierto nivel educativo y cierto capital cultural pudieron satisfacer las exigencias de las agencias financiadoras. Por ello, se ha constatado que las ONG's ofrecen una perspectiva profesional fuera del mercado de trabajo tradicional y de autorrealización a mujeres especialmente eruditas y generalmente provenientes de las clases media y alta*).
> (72)

It would be interesting, indeed, to learn why the work of these NGOs has done little in comparison to the scope of the problems. Do these women who are employed in the organizations not understand the true plight of working class and indigenous women? Or are the organizations and budgets too small to reach the diaspora of marginalized women?

Again, we can't be surprised to see that "common" Mexican women are totally in the dark in terms of what is done in the academic world or a world that doesn't extend to them. We could say that the feminist movement appears elitist, with a multitude of research and theory while possessing no praxis at all. Lang continues and supports our concern:

> the well-known feminists only represent a very small part of the female population in Mexico, very homogenous in its composition: like in the early days of feminist groups, it is again exclusively well educated, mestizo and white women who stem from middle and upper urban classes (*En los hechos, las conocidas feministas solo representan a una parte muy pequeña de la población femenina de México, muy homogénea en su composición: como en las primeras horas de los grupos feministas, se trata nuevamente casi exclusivamente de mujeres mestizas y blancas, eruditas y de las clases media y alta urbanas*).
> (73)

The women Lang writes about who don't share any oddities with the "common" women in the country are in their majority urban, well educated, mid and high class. They belong to a minority of women who may have more chances to participate openly in different areas of society, and also have more opportunities for upward mobility. These are the very limitations for poor indigenous women – maids and factory workers with a low educational level and poor cultural knowledge who are out of touch with the feminist movement.

Marta Lamas,[5] a long time well-known Mexican professor and feminist, published an interesting series of essays in her book *Feminism: Transmissions and Retransmissions* in which she seeks "to reach those who are thinking and debating about the kind of society we wish to build, and second, to reach those who are taking action on a daily basis to build this other kind of society" (xxi). Lamas writes about feminist movements in Latin America in general and specifically in Mexico. Throughout her essays the author focuses on the theoretical and philosophical standing of the feminist movement within academia and those with research backgrounds and expertise on the topic. We see, however, that there is also a gap between theory and praxis. Lamas mentions that some intellectuals of the feminist movement have reached out to the "common" women, such as those that belong to the Zapatista Movement whose army of women "issued their own bill of women's rights, detailing discriminatory practices, including those within indigenous communities, where they were often excluded from decision-making" (6). This Zapatista women's bill of rights and emancipation, however, wasn't born out of an academic activity, but from their own necessities within their particular patriarchal political and social context. Like working-class women in the country, indigenous women are disfranchised from the feminist upper class and intellectual movement that exerts little influence on them. A vast number of essays and critical articles sprout out of Lamas's book in the academic world. It is significant, nevertheless, that all of our interviewees have never heard of those essays and of such an important figure of the feminist movement since the 1970s and 1980s like Marta Lamas and others.

The interviews in this book with "common" Mexican women shed light on a variety of topics that have been and are always relevant to women's rights. Almost all of them agree that there have been some improvements for women in terms of education and jobs in both national and international companies. Maybe some of them were fortunate to have parents who were supportive of their wishes to pursue certain goals in their academic endeavors, and perhaps many other women were not so lucky; nevertheless, this is a positive change that will have an impact on women's lives in the country.

Even if machismo is still part of Mexico's cultural attributes, it appears that many men are becoming more concerned about women's rights and responsibilities and they would like to participate in a more egalitarian society. If access to education has seen improvement for women in Mexican society, it seems like sex out of wedlock is still not well accepted. Sex education at home is very important since it allows parents to teach their children, their daughters in this case, not to be afraid of their sexuality. Furthermore, mothers (and fathers) should exercise the right to teach their daughters about sex, pregnancies, sexually transmitted diseases, and other topics related to their children's sexuality. Only this way will their daughters learn about their own bodies and have a healthy sex life when they are ready. In Mexico, the sexual roles that women must play are still those of decades ago since they still do not share men's rights to enjoy their sexuality before marriage.

According to Alicia,

> Women in Mexico still lack sexual freedom to have the kind of life they would like; that is because we are still subject to opinions and social and religious perceptions about what women should or should not do about this issue. A woman is judged in a pejorative way; she might be called names such as a "bad" woman, even a prostitute many times. There is a very macho vision about this topic in the country.

In a country that prides itself on its Catholicism, sexual freedom is not something that society openly admits for women.

Certainly, a few interviewees had a close-knit relationship with their mothers who were supportive and always eager to offer an explanation about sexual topics raised by these women; a connection that many other women may not have enjoyed with their mothers. Like Clara, who sadly states:

> No, my mother never talked to me about my own sexuality; she wouldn't even think about talking to me about it. I remember that when I talked to my mother about menstruation, because they had talked to us about it in school, she slapped me in the face because I wasn't supposed to know about it.

Latin America in general, and Mexico in this particular case, are geographical places where most women outside of academia traditionally do not see themselves as feminists, yet they fight for their rights without subscribing to a feminist movement or discourse. That's why it is not surprising that at home many families do not see the need to talk about women's issues, but would rather talk about other daily social problems like poverty, corruption, drug cartels, politics in general, and the well-being of the family members. Karla, for instance, is very emphatic: "We don't talk directly about women's rights, not like an after-dinner topic."

Something is certain, however, in the sense that these interviewees wish for a better future for their daughters and their place in Mexican society; they wish for better treatment and better rights for them in a world of compassion, equal rights, responsibilities, and communication with men. Mexican women search, indeed, for an egalitarian future where their daughters share the same rights and responsibilities as men.

These interviews show how present-day Mexican women have (or have not) been influenced by the feminist movement in Mexico during the 1970s and 1980s, and by other women's fights for their rights in the years after. Although there have been some improvements in public education, for instance, there are still things to change in terms of education, female gender roles, religion, living under a patriarchal society, jobs, harassment in the workplace, sexual freedom, and the idea that men are the breadwinners in a family, just to mention a few issues.

These conversations do not demonstrate a similar pattern for all of Mexico. It would be wrong to think so in a nation of almost 50 million women. Yet they display a mosaic of what the Mexican feminist movement of the 1970s and 1980s did or did not achieve for "common" women in the nation. There are still those like Claudia who state about men and women:

> And each one has their own role; there are things that women can do and things that men can do, and things that women just can't do and well, we must accept that. I think that God created man for him to be perfect and God created woman to follow her own role.

This might be one of the reasons why "common" Mexican women face their own reality with sentiments such as we don't talk about feminism here.

Notes

1 Olivares, Cecilia. "Debatiendo sobre el feminismo en Mexico." *Revista Estudios Feministas*, 12 (septiembre–diciembre, 2004): 75–79. Universidade Federal de Santa Catarina, Santa Catarina, Brasil.
2 Cano, Gabriela. "Más De Un Siglo De Feminismo En México." *Debate Feminista* 14 (1996): 345–360.
3 Camarena Adame, Maria and Maria Luisa Saavedra Garcìa. "El techo de Cristal en México." *Revista de Estudios de Género, La Ventana E-ISSN: 2448-7724* 5, No. 47 (2018): 312–339. Online.
4 Lang, Miriam. "¿Todo el poder? Políticas públicas, violencia de género y feminismo en México." *Iberoamericana (2001–2003)*: 69–90.
5 Lamas, Marta. *Feminism: Transmissions and Retransmissions*. Trans. John Pluecker. Springer, 2011.

Index